**PRACTICE
MAKES
PERFECT**®

French
Problem Solver

Also by Annie Heminway

Practice Makes Perfect Complete French Grammar

Practice Makes Perfect French Pronouns and Prepositions

Practice Makes Perfect French Nouns and Their Genders Up Close

Practice Makes Perfect French Past-Tense Verbs Up Close

Practice Makes Perfect French Subjunctive Up Close

French Demystified

Better Reading French

PRACTICE MAKES PERFECT®

French Problem Solver

Annie Heminway

New York   Chicago   San Francisco   Athens   London   Madrid
Mexico City   Milan   New Delhi   Singapore   Sydney   Toronto

1 2 3 4 5 6 7 8 9 10 11 12 13 QVR/QVR 1 0 9 8 7 6 5 4 3

ISBN   978-0-07-179117-5
MHID   0-07-179117-5

e-ISBN   978-0-07-179119-9
e-MHID   0-07-179119-1

Library of Congress Control Number 2012947475

McGraw-Hill Education, the McGraw-Hill Publishing logo, Practice Makes Perfect, and
related trade dress are trademarks or registered trademarks of McGraw-Hill Education
and/or its affiliates in the United States and other countries and may not be used
without written permission. All other trademarks are the property of their respective
owners. McGraw-Hill Education is not associated with any product or vendor mentioned
in this book.

Interior design by Village Typographers, Inc.

McGraw-Hill Education products are available at special quantity discounts to use as
premiums and sales promotions or for use in corporate training programs. To contact a
representative, please e-mail us at bulksales@mcgraw-hill.com.

This book is printed on acid-free paper.

Contents

v

5 The past tenses 61

6 Future tense, conditional mood, and subjunctive mood • *Could, should, would* • *Whatever, whoever, wherever, whenever* 81

7 Verb transfers 100

Preface

Often perceived as a task, the business of learning a foreign language is neither a task nor a business: it is an adventure! It is just like the illuminating travels of Milo, the young protagonist of Norton Juster's incomparable book *The Phantom Tollbooth*. Many a learner of French has felt like Milo before his exciting journeys through the Kingdoms of Knowledge. "I can't see the point," laments Milo at the very beginning of the narrative, "in learning to solve useless problems, or subtracting turnips from turnips, or knowing where Ethiopia is or how to spell *February*."

Still, as every student of French knows, learning a foreign language can be an arduous, even maddening, task, despite many handy grammars, methods, and manuals. Indeed, there are times when a dedicated student's effort to solve a particular linguistic conundrum turns into the proverbial hunt for the needle in the haystack: "I know that the answer to my question is *somewhere* in my *Big French Grammar*, but I have no idea where it is; I feel like the astronomer who is struggling to identify the tiniest star in the largest galaxy."

Not to denigrate comprehensive grammars, for comprehensiveness is wonderful, but what makes *Practice Makes Perfect: French Problem Solver* indispensable is its selectiveness. Written for the English-speaking student of French, this particular problem-buster will identify and exorcise the particular grammatical poltergeists that habitually bedevil even advanced learners.

What seems to be the problem?

Often used, misused, and abused, the word *problem* conjures images of failure and frustration. Why does learning a language have to be problematic in the first place? In classical Greek, the word *problema* means, among many other things, "obstacle," as in literally "outcropping (of rock)." This less-threatening connotation is more appropriate for this book. A boulder blocking your way? Perhaps, but encountering an obstacle is never, at least in the process of learning a language, tantamount to reaching an impasse. At any rate, this book will teach you how to walk around those boulders. As this book unfolds, you will learn to transform problems into reliable knowledge.

The exercises in this book will be considerably less arduous than the obstacle course of études, scales, and arpeggios standing between an aspiring violinist and the technical expertise required for a concert career. Furthermore, while an instrumentalist's "answer key" is an unattainable ideal, your Answer Key (and Translations) will be right here, at the back of the book. So if you try to play a French scale, so to speak, and get stuck in the middle, you can look at the end result and then try again.

Remerciements

Merci!—to Mathilde Lauliac and Zoran Minderovic, my lynx-eyed readers, spirited spot-checkers, and punctiliously erudite French scholars.

Warmest thanks to my friend Dany Laferrière, whose immense talent is only matched by his generosity, for his beautiful prose contribution.

I am very grateful to Lisa Ehrenkranz for her witty message to Chloé—an inspiration for a future generation of Francophones—and to my other students: Gertrude Bernstein, Hannah Bismuth, Marie-Josée Charest, Melinda Chatain, Nathalie Chaudin, Janet Cohen, Hande Gizer, Ruth Gruenthal, Diane Howard, Michael Lotz, Bruce McCutcheon, Mary Kay Office, Valerie Pascale, Liz Salak, Ellen Sowchek, and Michelle Yu, who helped me identify the infinite hurdles, with their charming and imaginative essays which beautifully express the quirky, playful, and luminous spirit of the French language.

Last but foremost, thanks to Holly McGuire, my editor, for her expertise and invaluable support at every stage of this project and to Nancy Hall, senior project editor.

French
Problem Solver

Nouns: gender and pluralization

Gender and its intricacies

Gender demands special attention because it expresses the essential "being" of a word. Problems regarding gender require exceptional concentration and mental acuity. Fortunately, you will discover in this chapter a number of handy rules that will facilitate the task of recognizing and learning the correct gender of French words.

As you already know, there are two genders in French: masculine and feminine, preceded by the definite article **le, la**, or the indefinite article **un, une**. In the world of genders, fewer is better than more, so you should count your blessings if you sometimes find French genders exasperating—students of German have to struggle with three genders! Having inherited the neuter gender from Latin, French, in its infinite wisdom, decided to assign the masculine gender to most neuter nouns, which explains why one says **un argument** in French (derived from the Latin neuter noun *argumentum*).

In this chapter, you will learn that the seemingly arbitrary universe of French genders is not totally devoid of rhyme and reason. In other words, you will learn how to identify the correct gender of a noun by applying a handful of rules. However, these rules are not only limited but also have exceptions, which means that memorization remains the most reliable method. For example, when learning a new noun, never separate it from its gender marker (the definite or indefinite article). Simply knowing that **lune** means *moon* is not helpful: what you need to memorize is **la lune** so it remains etched in your memory like a melody.

The fundamental rule concerning gender is also the most obvious one: nouns denoting female beings are feminine. Be grateful for this rule because it is far from universal in the Indo-European family of languages. In German, for example, **das Mädchen** (*maiden*) is a neuter noun. No such nonsense in French: **la jeune fille** is unequivocally feminine. You can generalize this rule if you apply reasoning by analogy. For example, it is safe to assume that most nouns denoting a profession of or any activity performed by a woman will be feminine. Of course, exceptions exist. This is where the importance of noun endings comes to the fore, and some of these endings will be familiar to you because they belong to a legacy that English and French share. For example, we know that *abbess* is the feminine form of *abbot*. The French word for *abbess* is **abbesse**. If you peruse your dictionary, you will find many similar (and helpful) cognates.

Another typical feminine ending is **-ice** (from the Latin ending *-ix*), which occurs in words such as **institutrice**, the feminine form of **instituteur**, and means *teacher*. Numerous French words follow this pattern. Another very helpful pattern is found in the feminine ending **-ion**, which occurs in numerous French-English cognates, such as **nation**.

Of course, the realm of inanimate objects is quite different because gender assignment is, or seems, random. To a French speaker, **la lune** (*moon*) may seem naturally feminine, but in many cases the gender of an object defies explanation. Here, of course, we may rely on accepted conventions (e.g., cities are masculine) or even better, on word endings.

Genders are a big problem for the student of French, and the solution to this problem is the systematic memorization of particular categories of endings, with particular attention to exceptions. You may think that exceptions are annoying, but in French they add some spice and mystery to the task of memorization. For example, the ending **-ée** is generally feminine, as in **la soirée** (*evening*), but there are interesting exceptions, which include **le lycée** (*secondary school*). Now you can either fastidiously track down the origin of these masculine nouns in Latin neuter words (**le lycée** is derived from the Latin *lyceum*, which, like *argumentum*, is a neuter noun), or chalk the whole thing up to plain weirdness. For example, countries are generally feminine, but Canada is masculine. Either method works, as long as you remember the exceptions.

Basic masculine noun endings

Here are the basic masculine endings you must try and memorize:

-age	-ige	-ège	-oge	-uge
-ail	-eil	-euil	-ain	-al
-ament	-ement	-ard	-eau	-ou
-el	-ent	-ant	-er	-ier/yer
-at	-et	-t	-ien	-illon
-in	-is	-isme	-oir	-oin
-om	-phone	-scope	-ème	-me
-ome	-ble	-cle	-gle	-ple
-ac	-ak	-ic	-oc	-uc
-o	-op	-ort	-os	-ot
-ours	-us	-ogue	-x	-xe

As I've said, there are no rules without exceptions. So try to remember one ending at a time with a couple of exceptions, and then create a fun sentence that will stick in your mind.

For instance, the **-age** ending is masculine, but some exceptions are **la cage** (*cage*), **l'image** (*image*), **la nage** (*swimming*), **la page** (*page*), **la plage** (*beach*), **la rage** (*rage, fury, rabies*).

> **Le** mariage d'Aurélie et Fabien a eu lieu sur **la** plage d'**un** village en Bretagne.
> *Aurélie and Fabian's wedding took place on the beach of a village in Brittany.*

Words ending in **-ain** tend to be masculine, except **la main** (*hand*):

> Dans **le** train, Marc tenait **un** pain au chocolat d'**une** main, un livre de l'autre.
> *On the train, Marc held a chocolate croissant in one hand, a book in the other.*

Words ending in **-at**, **-et**, and **-t** tend to be masculine but here are some of the exceptions: **la nuit** (*night*), **la forêt** (*forest*), **la mort** (*death*), **la part** (*share*), **la plupart** (*most people*), **la dot** (*dowry*), **la basket** (*sneaker*).

> **La** protection de **la** forêt sera **le** sujet principal **du** débat ce soir.
> *The protection of the forest will be the main topic of the debate tonight.*

Basic feminine noun endings

Here are the basic feminine endings:

-ade	-aie	-aine	-aison	-oison
-ence	-ance	-ande	-éc	-esse
-osse	-ousse	-ette	-eur	-ie
-rie	-ise	-aille	-ille	-ouille
-ique	-gion	-nion	-sion	-ssion
-tion	-xion	-ite	-tié	-té
-ode	-ude	-ure		

Let's look at some endings and their exceptions. Words ending in **-ence** and **-ance** tend to be feminine, except **le silence** (*silence*):

> En dépit de **la** large audience, **la** conférence s'est déroulée dans **un** silence total.

> *Despite **the** large audience, **the** lecture took place **in** total silence.*

Words ending in **-ée** tend to be feminine, except **l'apogée** (*apogee, peak*), **l'athée** (*atheist*), **le lycée** (*high school*), **le musée** (*museum*), **le rez-de-chaussée** (*main floor*), **le trophée** (*trophy*), **le mausolée** (*mausoleum*). For example:

> Après **une** longue année d'études **au** lycée, les élèves vont passer **la** journée **au** musée du quai Branly.

> *After **a** long year of studying **at** their high school, **the** students are going **to** spend a day at the Quay Branly museum.*

Words ending in **-ie** and **-rie** tend to be feminine. Here are a few exceptions: **le génie** (*genius*), **l'incendie** (*fire*), **le parapluie** (*umbrella*), **le sosie** (*double*). For example:

> **Un** grave incendie a détruit **la** plus belle tapisserie du château.

> ***A** serious fire destroyed the most beautiful tapestry in **the** castle.*

EXERCICE 1·1

*Indicate the gender by adding the definite article **le** or **la**.*

1. _____ fauteuil de mon grand-père est près de la cheminée.

2. Regarde _____ grenouille sur la petite pierre!

3. Connais-tu _____ nationalité de Jack?

4. À la soirée, j'ai goûté _____ meilleur fromage du monde.

5. Ils passent leurs vacances sur _____ bateau de leurs voisins au large de Porquerolles.

6. Julie a été admise dans _____ lycée le plus convoité de Paris, près du Panthéon.

7. _____ différence de prix entre ces deux ordinateurs est énorme.

8. Allume _____ télévision! Le président va prononcer un discours.

9. Les campeurs se sont perdus _____ nuit dans _____ forêt.

10. Alice aime se promener dans _____ nature.

Indicate the gender by adding the indefinite article **un** *or* **une**.

1. Pourriez-vous me donner _____ conseil?

2. Hélène mange au moins _____ chocolat par jour.

3. L'économie mondiale traverse _____ grave récession.

4. Un entomologiste norvégien a trouvé _____ papillon rare.

5. Prends _____ parapluie! Le ciel est couvert.

6. Ils ont marché des heures sous _____ pluie battante.

7. Nathalie a eu _____ attitude déplorable pendant la réunion.

8. Vous recevrez _____ confirmation d'ici jeudi.

9. Les Vincent ont invité _____ vingtaine de personnes à dîner.

10. Valérie a acheté _____ hamac brésilien en ligne.

Gender and professions

As far as professions are concerned, the rules keep evolving and the feminization of names of professions formerly reserved for men is more common. However, you have to be careful, and you often need to check with the person in question whether she wants to be called **un** **ministre** or **une** **ministre**. Nothing is set. However, the following are the main rules.

In many cases, the noun of the profession is identical in the masculine and the feminine:

  un dentist**e**/une dentist**e**   *dentist*

Or you simply add an **-e** at the end of the noun:

  un avocat/une avocat**e**   *lawyer*

In other cases, there are many possible endings, depending on the noun:

  l'ouvri**er**/l'ouvri**ère**   *worker*
  le vend**eur**/la vend**euse**   *salesperson*
  le pharmac**ien**/la pharmac**ienne**   *pharmacist*
  le rédact**eur**/la rédact**rice**   *editor*
  le patr**on**/la patr**onne**   *boss*

Sometimes the two forms are different nouns:

  le roi/la reine   *king/queen*
  l'oncle/la tante   *uncle/aunt*
  le parrain/la marraine   *godfather/godmother*

Some nouns are the same when referring to a man or a woman:

le génie	*genius*
le mannequin	*model*
le témoin	*witness*

Some nouns are always feminine when referring to a man or a woman:

la célébrité	*celebrity*
la personne	*person*
la victime	*victim*

Gender and animals

As far as animals are concerned, the rule varies. Here are a few examples:

le chat/la chatte	*tomcat/female cat*
le chien/la chienne	*dog/bitch*
le lion/la lionne	*lion/lioness*
le coq/la poule	*rooster/hen*
le cheval/la jument	*horse/mare*

A large number of names of animals are epicene, meaning they work for either gender. To differentiate between the two sexes, you add *mâle* or *femelle*:

MASCULINE: cygne (*swan*), léopard (*leopard*), lézard (*lizard*), oiseau (*bird*), papillon (*butterfly*), perroquet (*parrot*), pigeon (*pigeon*).

FEMININE: autruche (*ostrich*), baleine (*whale*), chauve-souris (*bat*), crevette (*shrimp*), fourmi (*ant*), grenouille (*frog*), guêpe (*wasp*), hirondelle (*swallow*), libellule (*dragonfly*).

EXERCICE
1·3

Use the feminine form of the noun.

1. Il est traducteur. Elle est _____.

2. Il est roi. Elle est _____.

3. Il est informaticien. Elle est _____.

4. Il est infirmier. Elle est _____.

5. Il est mannequin. Elle est _____.

6. Il est parrain. Elle est _____.

7. Il est architecte. Elle est _____.

8. Il est marchand. Elle est _____.

9. Il est concepteur. Elle est _____.

10. Il est acheteur. Elle est _____.

Use the possessive adjective **son** *or* **sa**.

1. Colette était toujours photographiée avec _____ chatte grise.

2. Dany Boon, un des acteurs français les mieux payés, est _____ vedette préférée.

3. Les employés sont jaloux de _____ génie.

4. François 1er parcourait la France sur _____ célèbre cheval blanc.

5. _____ témoin principal doit se présenter au tribunal mardi.

6. Il s'est disputé avec _____ beau-père et _____ belle-mère.

7. Ce chanteur est devenu victime de _____ célébrité.

8. Zoé passera ses vacances chez _____ oncle et _____ tante.

9. _____ marraine lui a offert un bracelet en or.

10. Flaubert écrivait en compagnie de _____ perroquet Loulou.

What about geography?

Regions, provinces, and states ending in **-e** tend to be feminine. The others tend to be masculine with some exceptions, of course. Here are a few examples: **la Normandie, la Provence, la Champagne, la Californie, la Pennsylvanie, la Caroline-du-Sud,** but **le Limousin, le Languedoc, le Midi, le Michigan, le Vermont, le Colorado.**

Countries with an **-e** ending tend to be feminine. Other endings tend to be masculine: **la Chine, la France, la Russie, le Brésil, le Japon, le Sénégal.**

Watch out for the exceptions: **le Mexique, le Cambodge,** and so on.

Rivers have their own eccentric rules. Double-check all the time! Here are a few examples: **le Mississippi, le Rhône, le Mékong,** but **la Loire, la Volga, la Dordogne.**

Each category has a different set of rules: flowers, trees, fruit, vegetables, wine, cheese, cars, fabric, stones, days, months, seasons, holidays. Most flowers, fruits, and vegetables not ending in **-e** tend to be masculine. Most trees tend to be masculine. Names of wines and other alcoholic beverages, of cheeses, and of fabrics tend to be masculine. Precious stones can be either masculine or feminine, and in most cases, a car will be a feminine noun. Some nouns have the audacity to possess two possible genders! You can say *un* **après-midi** or *une* **après-midi** (*afternoon*), *un* **oasis** or *une* **oasis** (*oasis*). So memorize them in context.

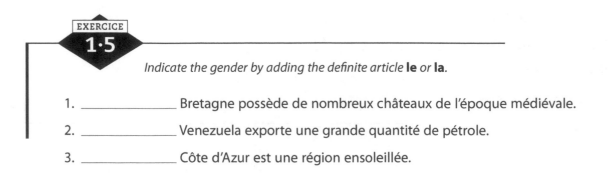

Indicate the gender by adding the definite article **le** *or* **la**.

1. _____ Bretagne possède de nombreux châteaux de l'époque médiévale.

2. _____ Venezuela exporte une grande quantité de pétrole.

3. _____ Côte d'Azur est une région ensoleillée.

4. _____ Thaïlande est un royaume connu pour ses danses traditionnelles et sacrées.

5. _____ Texas est célèbre pour ses champs de coton.

6. _____ Tanzanie accueille des réfugiés de nombreux pays.

7. _____ Japon est un archipel.

8. _____ Martinique est un département français dans la Caraïbe.

9. _____ Portugal a transformé bon nombre de ses palais en hôtels de luxe.

10. _____ Californie est le paradis des surfeurs.

11. _____ Chili est renommé pour son vin.

12. _____ Rhône et _____ Saône coulent dans la ville de Lyon.

13. _____ Suède est une destination privilégiée pour les sportifs, été comme hiver.

14. _____ Burkina Faso organise le plus grand festival de cinéma africain.

15. _____ Canada est le pays des grands espaces vierges.

16. _____ Mongolie propose des randonnées à cheval de yourte en yourte.

17. _____ Languedoc est une région où l'on parle encore occitan.

18. _____ Vietnam se caractérise par une population très jeune.

19. _____ Népal est un pays merveilleux accroché à l'Himalaya.

20. _____ Hongrie est entourée de nombreux voisins dont _____ Serbie et _____ Roumanie.

EXERCICE
1·6

Indicate the gender by adding the indefinite article **un** *or* **une**.

1. Matthieu lui a offert _____ rose rouge et _____ boîte de chocolats.

2. Sandrine vient d'acheter _____ Renault 5 jaune éclair.

3. Achète _____ camembert et _____ bleu d'Auvergne.

4. _____ rosé d'Anjou serait parfait pour accompagner cette blanquette de veau.

5. Il y a _____ petit cactus à l'entrée du magasin.

6. _____ satin de soie serait parfait pour sa robe du soir.

7. Ils nous ont servi _____ ananas avec de la glace.

8. Les Depardieu ont planté _____ olivier dans leur jardin.

9. Tu veux _____ orange ou _____ kiwi?

10. _____ des rosiers de Madame Germain est déjà en fleur.

Homographic homonyms

A large number of nouns are only differentiated by their gender. The spelling and the pronunciation are identical, but the meanings are different. It is most important to get acquainted with these homonyms to avoid any misunderstanding while reading or chatting with French people. Here are some examples:

MASCULINE		FEMININE	
le champagne	*champagne*	la Champagne	*Champagne region*
le critique	*critic*	la critique	*review, criticism*
le livre	*book*	la livre	*pound, pound sterling*
le manche	*handle*	la manche	*sleeve*
		la Manche	*the English Channel*
le mémoire	*MA thesis*	la mémoire	*memory*
le mode	*mode, way*	la mode	*fashion*
le page	*page (boy)*	la page	*page, episode*
le poêle	*heating stove*	la poêle	*frying pan*
le/la politique	*politician*	la politique	*politics*
le poste	*job, extension*	la poste	*post office*
le voile	*veil*	la voile	*sail, sailing*

Le manche du couteau est sale.
The **handle** of the knife is dirty.

La manche de sa chemise est tachée.
His shirt's **sleeve** is stained.

Mona a mis les pivoines dans **un** beau vase en cristal.
Mona put the peonies in a beautiful crystal **vase**.

Ils se sont retrouvés les pieds dans **la vase**.
They ended up with their feet in **slime**.

Homophonous homonyms

Homophonous homonyms are tricky. They are nouns pronounced in the same manner but that have different spellings and meanings. Some share the same gender. Others are either masculine or feminine. Let's look at a few examples in the masculine form and then in the feminine form. In the first set of examples, the gender is the same but the spelling is different.

l'amande (*f.*)	*almond*	l'amende (*f.*)	*fine*
l'autel (*m.*)	*altar*	l'hôtel (*m.*)	*hotel*
le champ	*field, domain*	le chant	*song*
le cœur	*heart*	le chœur	*choir, chorus*
l'encre (*f.*)	*ink*	l'ancre (*f.*)	*anchor*
le saint	*saint*	le sein	*breast, womb*
		le seing	*signature* (legal)
le saut	*jump, leap*	le sceau	*seal, stamp*
		le seau	*bucket*
		le sot	*fool*
la tache	*spot/stain*	la tâche	*task*
le ver	*worm*	le verre	*glass*
		le vers	*verse*
		le vert	*green*
la voie	*way/lane*	la voix	*voice*

Les enfants ont fait **une** belle **balade** le long de la mer.	*The children had a nice **walk** along the shore.*
Notre grand-mère nous a chanté **une** merveilleuse **ballade**.	*Our grandmother sang a wonderful **ballad** for us.*
On devrait faire **une pause** de trente minutes.	*We should take a thirty-minute **break**.*
Souris moins! Je n'aime pas **cette pose** pour la photo.	*Don't smile so much! I don't like the **way** you're **posing** for the camera.*

EXERCICE
1·7

*Complete with one of the nouns featured above, using the definite article **le** or **la**.*

1. _____ de maïs à droite appartient à M. Leconte.

2. _____ que Lucie doit écrire pour obtenir son diplôme ne peut pas dépasser 200 pages.

3. _____ est une région célèbre pour ses vignobles.

4. Donne-moi _____ en fonte pour faire des pommes de terres sautées.

5. _____ cet été, c'est des jupes courtes ou des jupes longues?

6. Je déteste _____ de ce chanteur. Ça me casse les oreilles.

7. _____ dans lequel vous buvez appartenait à ma grand-tante.

8. _____ de la cathédrale de Reims présentera son concert le 15 mai.

9. Un océanographe a retrouvé _____ d'un bateau naufragé au XIXe siècle.

10. _____ littéraire du Monde vient de massacrer le prix Goncourt.

EXERCICE
1·8

*Translate the following sentences, using **vous** if necessary.*

1. We stayed in a small hotel in the Marais.

_____

2. The green you chose for your curtains is too pale.

_____

3. This is an impossible task.

_____

4. My cousins Alain and Frédéric live in the heart of Paris.

_____

5. They served champagne with some almonds.

_____

6. There is a worm in this glass.

_____

7. Sara uses only blue ink.

_____

8. She had to pay a hundred-euro fine.

_____

9. Gregorian chant is sublime.

_____

10. Bring me a bucket of water right away!

_____

The pluralization of nouns

As in English, in French in most cases you simply add an **-s** to a noun to make it plural:

le chat (*cat*)   les chats (*cats*)
la tasse (*cup*)   les tasses (*cups*)

The plural ending of nouns in **-al** is **-aux**:

le journal (*newspaper*)   les journaux (*newspapers*)
l'animal (*animal*)   les animaux (*animals*)

Here are some exceptions: **les bals** (*bals*), **les carnavals** (*carnavals*), **les récitals** (*recitals*), **les festivals** (*festivals*).

To form the plural of nouns ending in **-eau** and **-eu**, an **-x** is usually added.

le manteau (*coat*)   les manteaux (*coats*)
le chapeau (*hat*)   les chapeaux (*hats*)
le jeu (*game*)   les jeux (*games*)
le neveu (*nephew*)   les neveux (*nephews*)

Here are some exceptions: **les pneus** (*tires*), **les bleus** (*shades of blue*).

The plural ending of nouns in **-ou** is **-ous**:

le cou (*neck*)   les cous (*necks*)
le kangourou (*kangaroo*)   les kangourous (*kangaroos*)

However, there are some key exceptions: **les bijoux** (*jewels*), **les cailloux** (*pebbles*), **les choux** (*cabbages*), **les genoux** (*knees*), **les hiboux** (*owls*), **les poux** (*lice*), **les joujoux** (*toys*).

If a noun ends in **-s**, **-x**, or **-z**, the noun remains the same in the plural:

le fils (*son*)	les fils (*sons*)
le bras (*arm*)	les bras (*arms*)
le prix (*price, award*)	les prix (*prices, awards*)
la voix (*voice*)	les voix (*voices*)
le nez (*nose*)	les nez (*noses*)
le gaz (*gas*)	les gaz (*gases*)

In the majority of cases, the pronunciation of the nouns does not change between the singular and the plural. Of course, there are some exceptions when the final consonant is pronounced in the singular but not in the plural:

le bœuf (*ox*)	les bœufs (*oxen*)
l'œuf (*egg*)	les œufs (*eggs*)
l'os (*bone*)	les os (*bones*)

EXERCICE

1·9

Put the following words in the plural form.

1. Ces (bateau) _____ font des croisières sur le Rhin.

2. Pour ce psychologue, ce sont des (cas) _____ difficiles à résoudre.

3. Les (prix) _____ augmentent sans cesse!

4. Les (Hindou) _____ célèbrent Holi, la fête des couleurs, début mars.

5. Bien que son père soit vétérinaire, elle a peur des (animal) _____.

6. Jean a marché de longues heures. Il a mal aux (genou) _____.

7. Nous cherchons de plus grands (local) _____ pour notre entreprise.

8. Les (feu) _____ d'artifice commencent à 21 heures pile.

9. Cédric a été élevé par des (nounou) _____ irlandaises.

10. Ce magasin vend des (bois) _____ exotiques très chers pour faire des meubles.

The pluralization of compound nouns

You have just studied the plurals of nouns—simple nouns. Of course, there are some compound nouns made of two or more words. There are rules, but as usual, there are exceptions as well.

When a compound noun is made of two nouns, one noun and an adjective, or two adjectives, in 99 percent of the cases they are both pluralized:

un chou-fleur (*cauliflower*)	des choux-fleurs (*cauliflowers*)
un bateau-mouche (*river boat*)	des bateaux-mouches (*river boats*)

un coffre-fort (*safe*)	des coffres-forts (*safes*)
un sourd-muet (*deaf-mute*)	des sourds-muets (*deaf-mutes*)
un grand-père (*grandfather*)	des grands-pères (*grandfathers*)
une belle-fille (*daughter-in-law*)	des belles-filles (*daughters-in-law*)

When a compound noun is made of one verb or adverb plus one noun, the verb or adverb remains in the singular and the noun is pluralized:

un haut-parleur (*loudspeaker*)	des haut-parleurs (*loudspeakers*)
une demi-journée (*half-day*)	des demi-journées (*half-days*)
un couvre-lit (*bedspread*)	des couvre-lits (*bedspreads*)

However, abstract nouns and nouns denoting an indivisible entity are not pluralized:

un abat-jour (*lampshade*)	des abat-jour (*lampshades*)
un gratte-ciel (*skyscraper*)	des gratte-ciel (*skyscrapers*)
un chasse-neige (*snowplow*)	des chasse-neige (*snowplows*)
un coupe-faim (*appetite suppressant*)	des coupe-faim (*appetite suppressants*)

When a compound noun is made of two nouns connected with the preposition **de**, only the first noun is pluralized:

| un chef-d'œuvre (*masterpiece*) | des chefs-d'œuvre (*masterpieces*) |
| un jet d'eau (*fountain, spray*) | des jets d'eau (*fountains, sprays*) |

When a compound noun is made of two nouns connected with the preposition **à**, both nouns remain in the singular form.

| un tête-à-tête (*private conversation*) | des tête-à-tête (*private conversations*) |
| un tête-à-queue (*spin, gyration*) | des tête-à-queue (*spins, gyrations*) |

This rule doesn't always work. Sometimes, two plural forms are accepted, like **des tire-bouchon** or **des tire-bouchons** (*corkscrews*), so always check the most current dictionary and do not be surprised if you find some discrepancies.

When a compound word includes a word ending in **-o**, the word in **-o** remains in the singular:

| Anglo-Saxon (*Anglo-Saxon*) | Anglo-Saxons (*Anglo-Saxon*) |
| Franco-Américain (*French-American*) | Franco-Américains (*French-American*) |

Proper names, as a rule, are not pluralized:

Les Lambert habitent au rez-de-chaussée.	*The Lamberts live on the main floor.*
Connaissez-vous les frères Goncourt?	*Do you know the Goncourt brothers?*
Les Diderot n'existent plus aujourd'hui.	*There are no more Diderots today.*
Trois Picasso viennent d'être vendus.	*Three Picassos were just sold.*
Les Fournier ont deux Renault rouges.	*The Fourniers have two red Renaults.*

Put the following words in the plural form.

1. coupe-vent _____

2. eau-de-vie _____

3. passe-partout _____

4. aide-mémoire _____

5. gratte-ciel _____

6. arrière-petite-fille _____

7. demi-litre _____

8. hors-d'œuvre _____

9. face-à-face _____

10. beau-frère _____

Accents, h aspiré, and capitalization

Accent on accents

There is an annoying tendency, quite widespread in the English-speaking world, to dismiss French accents as another example of Gallic eccentricity. In fact, there are reference sources, whose publishers shall remain unnamed, containing thousands of titles, without accents, of French-language publications. French accents are a nuisance, these publishers maintain, and what counts is correct spelling. Indeed, but while we're talking about correct spelling, let us remind the anti-accent crowd that the result of removing a needed accent is a *typo*.

As we shall see, French accents, which by the way have nothing to do with stress, not only indicate the *correct pronunciation* of a vowel, but also act as *semantic markers*. For example, consider the following two exclamations:

> Vivre . . . ou . . . ?
> Vivre . . . où . . . ?

They may sound the same, but their meaning is completely different. The first phrase, which might remind us of the dilemma expressed in Hamlet's famous soliloquy, could be translated as: *To live . . . or to . . . ?*

Perhaps expressing some confusion, but definitely lacking any sinister overtones, the second phrase means: *To live . . . where . . . ?*

Or imagine getting a photograph of a friend at the Louvre Pyramid in Paris. Without the necessary accent, the caption would read:

> Marie a la pyramide du Louvre.

This literally means: *Marie has the Louvre Pyramid.*

Without the **accent grave**, **a** is the third-person singular of the verb **avoir**; when we add the **accent grave**, as in **à**, we get a preposition! Now you know why people who denigrate French accents are not to be trusted.

There are four accents in French for vowels and a cedilla for the consonant **c**. In most cases, their main purpose is to modify the pronunciation of a vowel, except for the cedilla, of course, which modifies the pronunciation of a consonant.

É

The **accent aigu** (*acute accent*) **é** is used only with the vowel **e**, as in **été** (*summer*), and it indicates that the vowel should be pronounced as a *closed e*. Think of the *e* in the English word *bed*. Here are other examples:

14

le café	*coffee*
le céléri	*celery*
le désir	*desire*
l'épaule	*shoulder*
gérer	*to manage, to handle*
le médecin	*doctor*
le mélange	*mix*
le musée	*museum*
la poésie	*poetry*
la sécheresse	*drought*

In some words the initial **é** replaces an initial **s** that figures in earlier Latin and Old French forms. Note that the Latin **s** is still alive in the English cognates. Let's look at a few examples:

l'éponge	*sponge*
l'état, l'État	*state, condition*
l'étudiant	*student*
étudier	*to study*

È

The **accent grave** (*grave accent*) **è** is used on the vowels **a**, **e**, and **u**, as in **à** (*at, in*) and **mère** (*mother*), and has a more open pronunciation. For example, **è** resembles the vowel sound in the English word *bad*. (If you ever meet someone from Geneva, Switzerland, ask him or her to pronounce the name of that city: Genève. You will hear a deliciously open vowel in the second syllable.) Let's look at other examples:

à	*at, in*
après	*after*
la/la collègue	*colleague*
le congrès	*congress, conference*
la crème	*cream*
la grève	*strike*
l'interprète	*interpreter*
là	*here, there*
où	*where*
le procès	*lawsuit*

Circumflex

The **accent circonflexe** ˆ (*circumflex*) can be found on **a**, **e**, **i**, **o**, and **u**:

Le chien s'amuse avec un bâton.	*The dog plays with a stick.*
Ils ramassent des champignons dans la forêt.	*They pick mushrooms in the woods.*
Un touriste finlandais est tombé dans un abîme dans les Alpes.	*A Finnish tourist fell into an abyss in the Alps.*
Les hôtes sont arrivés en retard.	*The guests arrived late.*
Cette pêche n'est pas mûre.	*This peach is not ripe.*

If the English cognate contains an **s** that is missing in the French word, you may assume that the French word will need a circumflex accent, which fills the space created by the disappearance of the **s** in French. Most of these words, as you may have guessed, are derived from Latin. For example:

le coût	*cost*
la fête	*feast*
la forêt	*forest*
l'hôpital	*hospital*
l'hôte	*host*
l'intérêt	*interest*
la pâte	*pasta*

It is important to identify the meaning of words. Look at the examples:

- **a** versus **à**
Il **a** un nouvel ordinateur.	*He **has** a new computer.*
Il habite **à** Strasbourg.	*He lives **in** Strasbourg.*

- **de** versus **dé**
Elle est revenue **de** Turquie.	*She came back **from** Turkey.*
Les enfants jouaient aux **dés** dans la rue.	*The children played **dice** on the street.*

- **du** versus **dû**
Tu veux **du** thé ou **du** café?	*Do you want **some** tea or coffee?*
Ils ont **dû** partir à six heures.	*They **had to** leave at 6 o'clock.*

Diaeresis

Another accent is the **tréma**, or *diaeresis*. The diaeresis is used when two vowels are next to each other and the accented vowel represents a separate sound. In other words, both vowels in a diphthong must be articulated. For example:

aïe	*ouch*
ambiguïté	*ambiguity*
archaïque	*archaic*
bonsaï	*bonsai*
Caraïbe	*Caribbean*
coïncidence	*coincidence*
égoïste	*selfish*
faïence	*earthenware*
héroïne	*heroine*
laïc	*secular*
maïs	*corn*
mosaïque	*mosaic*
naïve	*naive*
Noël	*Christmas*

La cédille

There is also a graphic sign called **la cédille**, **ç**. The **cédille** (*cedilla*) is found only under the letter **c** before the vowels **a**, **o**, and **u**. It changes the hard sound of **catalogue** (*catalog*) (like a **k**) into a soft sound of **ça** (*this, that*). It is not used with the vowels **e** and **i**.

la balançoire	*swing*
le commerçant	*shopkeeper, merchant*
la façade	*façade, front*
la façon	*way, manner*
français	*French*

le garçon	*boy*
le glaçon	*ice cube*
la leçon	*lesson*
le reçu	*receipt*
le soupçon	*suspicion*

It is important to remember to use the **cédille** when conjugating verbs in different tenses:

nous commençons	*we start*
elle a aperçu	*she noticed*
en remplaçant	*while replacing*
il menaçait	*he was threatening*
nous plaçons	*we are placing*
je soupçonne	*I suspect*
tu déplaçais	*you moved*
ils enfonçaient	*they pushed, hammered*
je conçois	*I conceive, imagine*
il pinça	*he pinched*

EXERCICE
2·1

Choose the right form of the verb.

1. La journaliste annonçait/annoncait/annonssait les résultats de l'élection quand il y a eu une panne d'électricité.

2. Nous voyagons/voyageons/voyageeons en Sicile chaque automne.

3. Vous reconnaîssez/reconnaissez/reconnaiçez votre erreur.

4. Après la fête, mes amis rangèrent/rangerent/rangairent la maison très vite.

5. Élodie manga/mangai/mangea une crème brûlée.

6. Tu as été réveillé/reveillé/rêveillé par le chant du coq.

7. Je reconnaitrais/reconnaîtrais/reconnaîtrait la chanson si vous la chantiez.

8. Tous les étés, nous finançons/financons/finanssons une bibliothèque mobile.

9. J'ai enfin recu/ressu/reçu ma commande de livres.

10. Les associations écologiques empêchèrent/empecherent/empéchèrent le départ du vieux bateau.

EXERCICE
2·2

Restore the accents or the graphic signs in the following passage. (See Translations *at the back of this book for the English.)*

La porte etroite, André Gide (1909)

—Tiens! Ma porte n'etait donc pas fermee? dit-elle.

—J'ai frappe ; tu n'as pas repondu, Alissa, tu sais que je pars demain?

Elle ne repondit rien, mais posa sur la cheminee le collier qu'elle ne parvenait pas a agrafer. Le mot: fiancailles me paraissait trop nu, trop brutal, j'employai je ne sais quelle periphrase a la place. Des qu'Alissa me comprit, il me parut qu'elle chancela, s'appuya contre la cheminee . . . mais j'etais moi-meme si tremblant que craintivement j'evitais de regarder vers elle.

J'etais pres d'elle et, sans lever les yeux, lui pris la main; elle ne se degagea pas, mais, inclinant un peu son visage et soulevant un peu ma main, elle y posa ses levres et murmura, appuyee a demi contre moi:

—Non, Jerome, non; ne nous fiancons pas, je t'en prie . . . [. . .]
—Pourquoi?
—Mais c'est moi qui peux te demander: pourquoi? pourquoi changer?
Je n'osais lui parler de la conversation de la veille, mais sans doute elle sentit que j'y pensais, et, comme une reponse a ma pensee, dit en me regardant fixement:
—Tu te meprends, mon ami: je n'ai pas besoin de tant de bonheur. Ne sommes-nous pas heureux ainsi?
Elle s'efforcait en vain a sourire.
—Non, puisque je dois te quitter.
—Ecoute, Jerome, je ne puis te parler ce soir . . . Ne gatons pas nos derniers instants . . . Non, non. Je t'aime autant que jamais; rassure-toi. Je t'ecrirai; je t'expliquerai. Je te promets de t'ecrire, des demain . . . des que tu seras parti. Va, maintenant!

The h aspiré

In the French language, about 1,500 words start with the letter **h**. And of these, three hundred of them are called **h aspiré**.

You are acquainted with nouns like **l'habitant** (*inhabitant*), **l'habitude** (*habit*), **l'hélicoptère** (*helicopter*), **l'heure** (*hour, time*), **l'histoire** (*history, story*), **l'hiver** (*winter*), **l'homme** (*man*), **l'hôpital** (*hospital*), **l'hôtel** (*hotel*), **l'huile** (*oil*), and so on. These nouns start with an **h** that is silent and the article that precedes them needs an apostrophe.

The **h aspiré** is also silent, but the liaison between the article and the noun is not allowed, so there is no apostrophe on the article. Here are some of the most important nouns with **h aspiré**:

la haie	hedge
la haine	hatred
le hamac	hammock
le hameau	hamlet
la hanche	hip
le handicap	handicap
le haricot	bean
le hasard	chance
le harcèlement	harassment
la hausse	increase, rise
le haut	top, summit
le héros	hero
la hiérarchie	hierarchy
le homard	lobster
la honte	shame
le hors-d'œuvre	hors-d'oeuvre

This is of the utmost importance, for you don't want the French laughing at you when they hear: **les héros de la Révolution**, which when pronounced without the aspiration sounds like "The zeros (dummies) of the Revolution"!

As we've seen before, rules can be unreliable, so it's better to remember words in context.

EXERCICE

2·3

Using the preceding vocabulary list of **h aspiré** *words, translate the following sentences using the* **est-ce que** *form and* **tu** *when necessary.*

1. The hierarchy in this organization is a game of chance.

   _____

2. The hero of this new film is a man who lives in the hamlet next to our village.

   _____

3. The hatred between the two brothers is well-known.

   _____

4. Nora is surprised by the increase of the prices of the hotel's restaurant.

   _____

5. The hors-d'oeuvres they served were delicious.

   _____

6. Do you want to order the lobster on the menu?

   _____

7. Carole's father fractured his hip last week.

   _____

8. The hammock in the garden is a gift from Laurent.

   _____

9. The cold winter in this city is the main handicap for our grandparents.

   _____

10. The shame of his defeat is hard to accept.

    _____

Capitalization

In French, the capitalization of words differs quite a bit from English capitalization. After all this business of "rules but no rules," *one rule* is pretty solid: capitalization is more frequent in English than it is in French. Let's look at a few examples.

Nationalities

Adjectives that refer to nationalities are capitalized in English but not in French. Nouns that refer to nationalities are capitalized in both languages. For example:

Marie est **française**.	*Marie is **French**.*
Paolo est **brésilien**.	*Paolo is **Brazilian**.*
Son professeur est un **Français** de Lyon.	*Her teacher is a **Frenchman** from Lyon.*
Elle partage un appartement avec une **Italienne**.	*She shares her apartment with an **Italian woman**.*

Languages

Languages are capitalized in English but not in French. For example:

Ils apprennent l'**arabe**.	*They are learning **Arabic**.*
Nous parlons **espagnol** à la maison.	*We speak **Spanish** at home.*

Locations

When you write an address, the words for street, avenue, place, and other names for roads are not capitalized. For example:

25, rue de l'Université
55, avenue de Neuilly
110, boulevard des Capucines
37, quai Branly
1, place des Abbesses
7, impasse de la Tonnelle

Dates, time, days, months, and seasons

Such words are not capitalized. For example:

Son anniversaire est le 23 **août**.	*His birthday is on the 23rd of **August**.*
Nous partirons le 5 **décembre**.	*We'll leave on **December** 5.*
Paris, le 10 **mars** 2013	*Paris, **March** 10, 2013*
Il est 10**h**05.	*It is 10:05 **a.m.***

Religions

In French, the names of religions tend not to be capitalized except l'**Islam** (Islam):

le christianisme	*Christianity*
le judaïsme	*Judaism*
le bouddhisme	*Buddhism*
l'hindouisme	*Hinduism*

Geographic nouns

Geographic names, as we have seen at the beginning of this chapter, are capitalized: **l'Asie** (*Asia*), **l'Europe** (*Europe*), **les États-Unis** (*United States*), **la Loire** (*Loire River*), **La Nouvelle-Orléans** (*New Orleans*), **La Havane** (*Havana*), **Aix-en-Provence** (*Aix-en-Provence*).

If the geographic noun is composed of a generic name (*bay*, *cape*, *river*, *sea*, etc.) and a specific noun, only the specific noun is capitalized:

la mer Rouge	*the Red Sea*
la mer Noire	*the Black Sea*
la mer Morte	*the Dead Sea*
l'île Maurice	*Mauritius Island*
l'île de Ré	*Île de Ré*
la baie des Anges	*the Bay of Angels*
le cap Horn	*Cape Horn*
la péninsule Ibérique	*the Iberian Peninsula*
le désert d'Arabie	*the Arabian Desert*
l'océan Pacifique	*the Pacific Ocean*
le pôle Nord	*the North Pole*

You will run into many other cases like **l'Asie centrale** (*Central Asia*), **l'Asie Mineure** (*Asia Minor*), **l'Asie du Sud-Est** (*Southeast Asia*), **l'Arabie Saoudite** (*Saudi Arabia*), **le Moyen-Orient** (*the Middle East*), **l'Extrême-Orient** (*the Far East*), **les Grands Lacs** (*the Great Lakes*), so check your dictionary.

EXERCICE
2·4

*Translate the following sentences. Be aware of the capitalization of words, using **tu** when necessary.*

1. Jean is Belgian.

_____

2. Isabella is Hungarian.

_____

3. Bruno's children speak French with their friends and English with their parents.

_____

4. In Greece, winter is mild.

_____

5. Lucie was born on February 28.

_____

6. The jazz festival takes place from July 1 to 4.

_____

7. The Mediterranean Sea is less salty than the Dead Sea.

_____

8. Spanish and Portuguese are the main languages in Latin America.

_____

9. The South Pole is in the Antarctic.

_____

10. When you are skiing in the Alps, you can go from France to Slovenia.

_____

Addressing people

When writing to people in French, capitalize most titles:

> Monsieur Verneuil
> Madame Deneuve
> Maître Didier Lebon
> Monsieur le Recteur de l'académie de Poitiers
> Monsieur le Premier ministre

Accents on capitals

An old topic for debate: are accents needed on capitals? Although there is still some disagreement, it is *absolutely necessary* to use accents on capitals to avoid misinterpretation. Here are a few examples of headlines in a newspaper. You'll see how including accents makes a significant difference!

A NANTES, UN ASSASSIN TUE.	*IN NANTES, A MURDERER KILLS.*
À NANTES, UN ASSASSIN TUÉ.	*IN NANTES, A MURDERER IS KILLED.*
PAUL EST INTERNE A L'HOPITAL.	*PAUL IS AN INTERN IN THE HOSPITAL.*
PAUL EST INTERNÉ À L'HÔPITAL.	*PAUL IS CONFINED IN THE MENTAL HOSPITAL.*

And for another reason, it is simply more elegant in prose. It's a question of pure aesthetics. Just take a look:

> Étant donné la promotion d'Air France pour les vols à destination des États-Unis, Ève et
> Édouard ont décidé de passer une semaine à la Nouvelle-Orléans.
> *Given the Air France promotion for flights to the USA, Ève and Édouard have decided to spend
> a week in New Orleans.*

So, all to your keyboards!

Adjectives and adverbs   ·3·

Adjectives

It would be impossible to imagine a language without adjectives—the words that describe nouns. Without adjectives, no text could tell us whether Arielle's house is tall or purple, huge or miniscule. In fact, if we didn't have Arielle's picture, we wouldn't know what she looked like. While English adjectives know their place (usually preceding the noun) and Latin adjectives do as they please, French adjectives may dance around the noun, slightly exasperating the learner. Luckily, this is not a tarantella, for French has rules that are capable of reining in unruly adjectives.

In most cases, a French adjective follows the noun that it modifies. But underneath that apparent regularity, one perceives an extraordinary synergy of noun and adjective, which comes to the fore when the adjective, moving to a different spot, not only modifies the image that the noun represents but also transforms its meaning. Great masters of French prose, such as Balzac and Flaubert, have used adjectives to illuminate the finest nuances of meaning in a phrase. Consider, for example, the difference between the following:

un meuble **ancien**	an **antique** piece of furniture

and

leur **ancien** patron	their **ex**-boss
ma **propre** voiture	my **own** car

and

ma voiture **propre**	my **clean** car

A few adjectives, like the preceding, change meaning depending on whether they are placed before or after the noun. We'll discuss them later in this chapter.

Before proceeding, we should introduce a fundamental problem-solving rule regarding adjectives. Nouns and adjectives are symbiotic creatures. An adjective standing alone is mute. Always look at an adjective-noun pair in the context of a *phrase*; use the *phrase* to find out what exactly an adjective is doing in a sentence.

Formal features of adjectives

Let us study the formal features of adjectives. First of all, they agree in gender and number with the noun they modify. One general rule is to add an **-e** to the masculine form of an adjective to make the feminine form. If a masculine adjective ends with an **-e**, it works for both genders.

Cet immeuble est très **grand**.	*This building is very **big**.*
Cette maison est très **grande**.	*This house is very **big**.*
Ce garçon est **intelligent**.	*This boy is **smart**.*
Cette fille est **intelligente**.	*This girl is **smart**.*

The preceding rule is general but not universal, which means that in French feminine adjectives can be formed in many different ways. For example:

Antoine est **parisien**.	*Antoine is **Parisian**.*
Églantine est **parisienne**.	*Églantine is **Parisian**.*
Ce gâteau est **délicieux**.	*This cake is **delicious**.*
Cette confiture est **délicieuse**.	*This jam is **delicious***
Aurélien est **curieux**.	*Aurélien is **curious**.*
Cécile est **curieuse**.	*Cécile is **curious**.*
Lucas est **naïf**.	*Lucas is **naïve**.*
Colombe est **naïve**.	*Colombe is **naïve**.*
Ce sont de **faux** papiers.	*These are **forged** papers.*
C'est une **fausse** alerte.	*It is a **false** alarm.*

You probably noticed the following masculine/feminine pairs of endings in the preceding phrases: **-ien/-enne, -eux/-euse, -ïf/-ïve, -aux/-ausse**. Many such pairs exist in French. Despite the inevitable exception, it is imperative to learn these patterns.

Of course, like nouns, adjectives can also be irregular. Consider these examples:

Le temps est **beau**.	*The weather is **nice**.*
La mariée est **belle**.	*The bride is **beautiful**.*
Ce savant est **fou**.	*This scientist is **mad**.*
Cette idée est **folle**.	*This idea is **crazy**.*
Notre nouveau chat est **blanc**.	*Our new cat is **white**.*
Notre nouvelle maison est **blanche**.	*Our new house is **white**.*
Ce bureau est trop **cher**.	*This desk is too **expensive**.*
Cette chaise est trop **chère**.	*This chair is too **expensive**.*
Erwan est **breton**.	*Erwan is **from Britanny**.*
Mailys est **bretonne**.	*Mailys is **from Britanny**.*
C'est un **vieux** manuscrit.	*It is an **old** manuscript.*
C'est une **vieille** partition.	*It is an **old** score.*

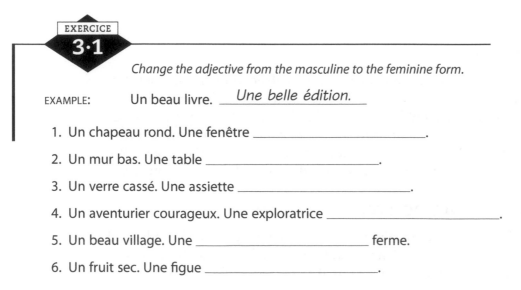

EXERCICE
3·1

Change the adjective from the masculine to the feminine form.

EXAMPLE: Un beau livre. _____*Une belle édition.*_____

1. Un chapeau rond. Une fenêtre _____.

2. Un mur bas. Une table _____.

3. Un verre cassé. Une assiette _____.

4. Un aventurier courageux. Une exploratrice _____.

5. Un beau village. Une _____ ferme.

6. Un fruit sec. Une figue _____.

7. Un film violent. Une tempête _____.

8. Un vieux pêcheur. Une _____ bergère.

9. Un jeune enfant. Une _____ vache.

10. Un voyage ennuyeux. Une tâche _____.

Plural forms of adjectives

Many adjectives add an **-s** to the singular form to create a plural form. This is a useful rule that you will have to quickly memorize and file away so you can focus on the most frequent irregular plural endings:

un livre **neuf**	a **new** book
des livres **neufs**	**new** books
un plat **épicé**	a **spicy** dish
des plats **épicés**	**spicy** dishes
une amie **belge**	a **Belgian** friend
des amies **belges**	**Belgian** friends
une route **enneigée**	a **snow-covered** road
des routes **enneigées**	**snow-covered** roads

Fortunately, irregular plurals are not random. Adjectives ending in **-s** or **-x** do not change in the plural:

un **grand** château	a **big** castle
de **grands** châteaux	**big** castles
un enfant **jaloux**	a **jealous** child
des enfants **jaloux**	**jealous** children

Most adjectives ending in **-al** change to **-aux**:

un résultat **normal**	a **normal** result
des résultats **normaux**	**normal** results
un ami **loyal**	a **loyal** friend
des amis **loyaux**	**loyal** friends

But for the feminine, only "s" is added. There is no change to "aux."

une note **finale**	a **final** grade
des notes **finales**	**final** grades

Some adjectives ending in -al change to -als:

un incident **banal**	a **banal** incident
des incidents **banals**	**banal** incidents
un accueil **glacial**	an **icy** welcome
des accueils **glacials**	**very cold** welcomes

Adjectives ending in **-eau** take an **-x** in the plural:

un frère **jumeau**	a **twin** brother
des frères **jumeaux**	**twin** brothers

un **beau** stylo	a **nice** pen
de **beaux** stylos	**nice** pens

Let's look at some foreign adjectives:

un rayon **gamma**	a **gamma** ray
des rayons **gamma**	**gamma** rays
une robe **sexy**	a **sexy** dress
des robes **sexy**	**sexy** dresses
une cape **chic**	a **chic** cape
des capes **chic**	**chic** capes
une chanson **pop**	a **pop** song
des chansons **pop**	**pop** songs
un jeu **vidéo**	a **video** game
des jeux **vidéo**	**video** games

EXERCICE
3·2

Change the adjective from the singular to the plural form.

1. Une grosse bêtise. De _____ gouttes.

2. Un voisin amical. Des collègues _____.

3. Une peinture murale. Des décorations _____.

4. Un patron mécontent. Des clients _____.

5. Un coup fatal. Des accidents _____.

6. Un chat roux. Des cheveux _____.

7. Un temps idéal. Des conditions _____.

8. Un maquillage waterproof. Des montres _____.

9. Une réaction normale. Des réactions _____.

10. Une transmission orale. Des communications _____.

Agreement rules

If all the nouns in a sentence are feminine, the adjective describing them should be in the feminine plural:

La tulipe et la pivoine sont **belles**.	*The tulip and the peony are **beautiful**.*
La machine à laver et la cuisinière sont **toutes neuves**.	*The washing machine and the stove are **brand-new**.*

If at least one of the nouns in a sentence is masculine, the adjective should be in the masculine plural. (Here's sexism in French grammar for you!) For example:

Le rideau et la fenêtre sont **ouverts**.
Pierre et Isabelle sont **intelligents**.
Monsieur et Madame Clémenceau
    sont très **gentils**.

The curtain and the window are **open**.
Pierre and Isabelle are **bright**.
Mr. and Mrs. Clémenceau are very **nice**.

EXERCICE
3·3

Complete with the correct form of the adjective.

1. Ma chambre a des murs et des fenêtres (bleu) _____.

2. Natacha a rassemblé les livres et les affiches (déchiré) _____.

3. La voiture avait deux vitres (brisé) _____ et une roue
   (crevé) _____.

4. Le cirque présente des éléphants et des lionnes très (talentueux) _____.

5. Les toits des maisons étaient (arrondi) _____ et
   (rouge) _____.

6. La mer était tantôt (bleu) _____ et
   (tranquille) _____, tantôt (gris) _____ et
   (déchaîné) _____.

7. Tu as offert des vêtements et des accessoires (neuf) _____ à ton ami.

8. Mathieu fait des listes de choses (utile) _____,
   (prévu) _____, ou (perdu) _____.

9. Valentin collectionne les timbres et les cartes postales (ancien) _____.

10. Les vitrines des magasins étaient (vide) _____,
    (rempli) _____, (multicolore) _____ ou
    (blanc) _____.

Compound adjectives

In compound adjectives, agreement between the adjectives and the noun depend on several structural, functional, and semantic factors. For example, if both adjectives forming the compound adjective qualify the same noun, they should both agree with that noun:

des sauces **aigres-douces**	*sweet-and-sour* sauces
des fils **premiers-nés**	*firstborn* sons

A notable exception would be a compound in which the first adjective ends in an **-o** or **-i**:

les traditions **anglo-saxonnes**	*Anglo-Saxon* traditions
des films **tragi-comiques**	*tragicomic* movies

If the compound contains an invariable adjective, only the other adjective agrees with the noun:

| une **avant-dernière** version | a *next-to-last* version |
| des étudiants **nord-américains** | *North American* students |

If the first adjective of the compound functions as an adverb, only the second adjective agrees with the noun:

| une tentative **mort-née** | a *stillborn* attempt |
| des hommes **tout-puissants** | *all-powerful* men |

EXERCICE
3·4

Complete with the correct adjective.

1. C'est une crème (anti-âge) _____.

2. As-tu mis un cadenas (antivol) _____ à ton vélo?

3. Les scientifiques ont signalé des signes (avant-coureur) _____ d'une éruption volcanique.

4. Au retour de l'école, Nicolas a retrouvé ses peluches (bien-aimé) _____.

5. Les bottes de Valentine sont (bicolore) _____.

6. Les déchets organiques sont (biodégradable) _____.

7. J'ai des cousins (casse-cou) _____.

8. Vous devriez acheter une carte (demi-tarif) _____.

9. Ces saladiers sont (interchangeable) _____.

10. Ces masques sont (subsaharien) _____.

Adjectives describing colors

Adjectives describing colors usually agree in gender and number with the noun they modify:

Les chats persans ont les yeux **bleus**.	Persian cats have **blue** eyes.
Pierre porte des chaussettes **jaunes**.	Pierre wears **yellow** socks.
À la pension, Ursula porte une jupe **grise**.	In boarding school, Ursula wears a **gray** (skirt).
Où as-tu mis ma casquette **bleue**?	Where did you put my **blue** cap?

Adjectives that are also the names of fruits, plants, or precious stones remain in the masculine singular form:

Tu as choisi des serviettes **émeraude**.	You have chosen **emerald-green** napkins.
Leurs robes sont **orange**.	Their dresses are **orange**.
Les jumelles portaient des cardigans **aubergine**.	The twin sisters wore **aubergine** cardigans.

Il est écrit sur mon passeport que j'ai
les yeux **marron**. Ce n'est pas vrai!

*My passport says that my eyes are **brown**.
It's not true!*

If two adjectives of color are combined to provide more specificity, both adjectives remain in the masculine singular form:

Les fleurs étaient **rose pâle**.
Manon a une écharpe **vert anis**.
Patrick porte des chemises **bleu clair**.
La mère de la mariée portait un
chapeau **jaune citron**.

*The flowers were **pale pink**.
Manon has an **anise-green** scarf.
Patrick wears **light blue** shirts.
The bride's mother was wearing a **lemon-
yellow** hat.*

EXERCICE
3·5

Complete each sentence with the correct adjective.

1. Au printemps, les fleurs du jardin sont (rose) _____, (mauve) _____ et (fuchsia) _____.

2. Leurs chemisiers étaient en soie (vert pâle) _____.

3. Elizée aime les fleurs (violet) _____ et les foulards (jaune) _____.

4. Au coucher du soleil, les nuages sont devenus (rose orangé) _____.

5. Ils ont navigué sur une mer (azur) _____.

6. Capucine a acheté un manteau (bleu canard) _____ et des gants (gris souris) _____.

7. Les murs des maisons italiennes sont (ocre) _____.

8. La nuit, tous les chats sont (gris) _____.

9. Nous avons mis les cerises et les oranges dans des saladiers (vert pomme) _____.

10. Le lit avait des draps (bleu foncé) _____ et une couverture (blanc) _____.

Expressions with colors

Human languages revel in color. Colors contribute a vital element to every type of discourse within the vast spectrum of human expression. A naturalist would be blind without the ability to describe the virtually limitless chromaticism of natural phenomena. Writers rely on color in a true synesthetic manner, even beyond the physical world. Deprived of color, the entire edifice of literary images, idioms, metaphors, and other figures of expression would relinquish much of its charm.

Despite certain English-French parallels (**voir rouge**, *see red*), once you leave the realm of archetypal color-based dichotomies, such as black-and-white, don't assume you can simply translate one way or the other. For example, a French person will be "green with fear," rather than "white with fear" as in the English idiom. You can gain much understanding by studying French cultural history, for as we know quite well, there is a story behind every color.

- ◆ **Expressions with white: une arme blanche** (*weapon with a blade*), **une page blanche** (*a blank page*), **un col blanc** (*white-collar worker*), **avoir carte blanche** (*to have a free hand*), **connu comme le loup blanc** (*well-known, a household name*), **montrer** (*to prove one is acceptable*), **se faire des cheveux blancs** (*to worry oneself*)
- ◆ **Expressions with dark colors: la matière grise** (*gray matter*), **être gris** (*to be tipsy*), **éminence grise** (*éminence grise*), **broyer du noir** (*to be down in the dumps*), **l'or noir** (*oil*), **un petit noir** (*a cup of coffee*)
- ◆ **Expressions with yellow: le maillot jaune** (*the leader in the Tour de France wears the yellow jersey*), **le nain jaune** (*pope Joan* [a card game]), **franchir la ligne jaune** (*to cross the line*)
- ◆ **Expressions with green: le billet vert** (*the dollar bill*), **vert de peur** (*to be green with fear* [comparable to "white with fear" in English]), **avoir la main verte** (*to have a green thumb*), **donner le feu vert** (*to give the green light*), **petits hommes verts** (*little green men*), **un vert** (*an ecologist*), **vert de jalousie** (*green with envy*)
- ◆ **Expressions with red: voir rouge** (*to see red*), **le fil rouge** (*the red thread*), **la planète rouge** (*the red planet, Mars*), **un rouge** (*a communist*), **voir la vie en rose** (*to see life through rose-tinted spectacles*)
- ◆ **Expressions with blue: cordon bleu** (*esteemed chef*), **être fleur bleue** (*to be a romantic soul*), **la planète bleue** (*the earth*), **avoir une peur bleue** (*to be scared to death*)

Position of adjectives

In French, most qualifying adjectives follow the noun. Although this rule is general, frequently applied, and accurately defines the melody of the French language, it is not universal. The natural flow of French discourse often needs to be interrupted, muted, or intensified for dramatic effect. In many cases, a discrete noun-adjective reversal does the trick.

Descriptive and classificatory adjectives are used to describe (or identify) color, nationality, taste, appearance, style, and so on.

J'ai une voiture **rouge**.	*I have a **red** car.*
Laure a des ancêtres **irlandais**.	*Laure has **Irish** ancestry.*
C'est un fruit **sucré**.	*It is a **sweet** fruit.*
Nora, ton tailleur est **démodé**.	*Nora, your suit is **out-of-fashion**.*

Adjectives can also be predicative. While attributive adjectives define an object in the most concise way (*a blue lake*), predicative adjectives can be more elaborate:

C'est un enfant **facile à vivre**.	*It is an **easygoing** child.*
Dimitri pense que c'est un arbre **haut de quinze mètres**.	*Dimitri thinks that the tree is **fifteen meters high**.*

Adjectives can be used with adverbs:

Sofia aime les bijoux **trop voyants**.	*Sofia likes **gaudy** jewelry.*
Voici une ascension **extrêmement risquée**.	*This is an **extremely risky** ascent.*

A participle can function as an adjective:

C'est un chat **perdu**.	*It is a **lost** cat.*
C'est un jean **délavé**.	*These are **prewashed** jeans.*
Ce sont des idées **erronées**.	*These are **erroneous** ideas.*
Le manteau d'Éliane est **usé**.	*Éliane's coat is **worn out**.*

Adjectives preceding the noun

These adjectives often express appreciation and emotions. They tend to be short and include **autre** (*other*), **beau** (*beautiful*), **bon** (*good*), **gros** (*big, fat*), **joli** (*pretty, nice*), **vaste** (*large, vast*), **vieux** (*old*), **vilain** (*ugly, nasty*). Consider these examples:

C'est un **beau** bébé.	*He is a **beautiful** baby*
C'est une **petite** erreur.	*It is a **minor** mistake.*
C'est un **joli** tableau.	*It is a **nice** painting.*
Nous viendrons un **autre** jour.	*We will come **another** day.*

However, most short adjectives follow the noun: for example, **cru** (*raw*), **frais** (*fresh*), **froid** (*cold*), **laid** (*ugly*), **lisse** (*smooth*), **neuf** (*brand-new*), **sec** (*dry*), **sûr** (*sure*).

Ils voudraient des boissons **fraîches**.	*They would like **cool** drinks.*
J'adore les carottes **crues**.	*I love **raw** carrots.*
Je n'aime pas le temps **froid**.	*I don't like **cold** weather.*
Nous voulons un vin **sec**.	*We want a **dry** wine.*

Adjectives qualifying proper nouns are often placed before the noun for emphasis. Here are four stars from the movies, past and present:

La **célèbre** Marilyn Monroe.	*The **famous** Marilyn Monroe.*
L'**inoubliable** Jean Gabin.	*The **unforgettable** Jean Gabin.*
L'**irrésistible** Gérard Philipe.	*The **irresistible** Gérard Philipe.*
La **grandiose** Isabelle Huppert.	*The **grandiose** Isabelle Huppert.*

Here are some examples of numeral adjectives:

J'habite au **dernier** étage.	*I live on the **top** floor.*
Le **premier** trimestre est le plus difficile.	*The **first** term is the most difficult.*
Je te le dis pour la **dernière** fois!	*I am telling it to you for the very **last** time!*
Isabelle habite dans le **7ème** arrondissement.	*Isabelle lives in the **seventh** arrondissement.*

Before or after

Some adjectives either precede or follow the noun, and their position in the sentence modifies their meaning.

ancien	*old, former*
bas	*low*
brave	*brave, decent*
bref	*short, curt*
certain	*certain, some*
cher	*dear, expensive*
chaud	*hot*
court	*short*
cruel	*cruel, harsh*
curieux	*curious, strange*
doux	*sweet, gentle*
droit	*right, straightforward, righteous*
drôle	*funny, odd*
dur	*hard, difficult*
entier	*whole, full*
faux	*false, untrue, wrong*
fin	*fine, subtle, sharp*

fort	*strong, intense*
fou	*insane, wild, frantic*
futur	*future, prospective*
gentil	*nice, kind*
grand	*tall, large, eminent*
haut	*high, high-class*
heureux	*happy, fortunate*
humble	*humble, obscure*
jeune	*young, immature*
juste	*right, just, accurate*
large	*wide, vast, large*
long	*long*
lourd	*heavy, weighty, dull*
maigre	*thin, sparse, poor*
malin	*malignant, clever, sharp*
mauvais	*bad, unkind, wrong*
meilleur	*better, best*
même	*same, self*
mince	*thin, insignificant*
mou	*soft, languid*
nouveau	*new, another*
pâle	*pale, faint, light*
pauvre	*poor, unfortunate, meager*
plein	*full, solid, replete*
premier	*first, best, essential*
prochain	*nearest, next, imminent*
propre	*clean, decent, proper*
pur	*pure, innocent*
rare	*rare, unusual, sparse*
riche	*rich, prolific, fruitful*
sale	*filthy, unsavory*
seul	*alone, single*
simple	*simple, innocent, common*
tendre	*tender, delicate, soft*
triste	*sad, dreary*
unique	*single, only, unmatched*
vain	*vain, futile, trivial*
véritable	*true, good, genuine*
vrai	*true, authentic*

une **brave** fille	*a **nice** girl*
un homme **brave**	*a **brave** man*
un **certain** nombre d'erreurs	*a **certain** number of mistakes*
une femme d'un âge **certain**	*a woman of **advanced** years*
un échec **certain**	*a **definite** failure*
un **curieux** garçon	*a **strange** boy*
une fille **curieuse**	*a **curious** girl*
Cette expression a **différents** sens.	*This expression has **various** meanings.*
Tu lis un livre **différent** toutes les semaines.	*You read a **new** book every week.*
Où est ma chaussure **droite**?	*Where is my **right** shoe?*
une femme **droite**	*a **righteous** woman.*
un **grand** homme	*an **important** man*
un homme **grand**	*a **tall** man*

Victor n'est pas estimé à sa **juste** valeur.	*One does not recognize Victor's **real** worth.*
C'est une décision **juste**.	*It is a **fair** decision.*
Le **pauvre** chien restait dehors.	*The **poor** dog stayed outside.*
La Croix-Rouge aide les familles **pauvres**.	*The Red Cross helps **poor** families.*
Adèle viendra avec sa **propre** voiture.	*Adèle will come with her **own** car.*
Charles rangeait la vaisselle **propre**.	*Charles was putting the **clean** dishes away.*

EXERCICE 3·6

Match the fragments in the two columns to form complete sentences. Proceed by elimination to make sure there is only one logical answer possible.

_____ 1. Yasmine est

_____ 2. Louis XIV a vécu

_____ 3. Emmanuel est

_____ 4. Nous avons choisi

_____ 5. Le candidat réclamait

_____ 6. Ma boîte aux lettres est pleine

_____ 7. Clara rêve de rencontrer en personne

_____ 8. Mon unique costume propre

_____ 9. L'avocat a utilisé

_____ 10. Jonathan a obtenu

a. le célèbre Bartabas.

b. est au pressing.

c. d'enveloppes vides.

d. de mauvaises notes à l'examen de français.

e. des arguments contradictoires.

f. un homme élégant.

g. un canapé en cuir lisse.

h. une autre chance.

i. fille unique.

j. au seizième siècle.

Several adjectives together

If a noun is placed between two adjectives, their position isn't random. It is determined by usage and sonority. The placement of the adjective in the phrase **un petit oiseau** is dictated by usage. Consequently if another adjective is added to the phrase, it will follow the noun.

un **petit** oiseau	*a **small** bird*
un oiseau **noir**	*a **black** bird*
un **petit** oiseau **noir**	*a **small black** bird*
une **belle** armoire	*a **beautiful** cupboard*
une armoire **normande**	*a **Norman** cupboard*
une **belle** armoire **normande**	*a **beautiful Norman** cupboard*

If two adjectives precede or follow the noun, they must be separated by **et** or **mais**. For example:

un vélo **bleu**	*a **blue** bike*
un vélo **neuf**	*a **new** bike*

Adjectives and adverbs **33**

un vélo **bleu** et **neuf**	*a **new blue** bike*
une **belle** montre	*a **beautiful** watch*
une **grosse** montre	*a **big** watch*
une **belle** mais **grosse** montre	*a **beautiful** but **big** watch*

Some adjectives that usually precede the noun have a fixed order of appearance:

un **joli** sac	*a **lovely** bag*
un **petit** sac	*a **small** bag*
un **joli petit** sac	*a **lovely small** bag*
le **bon vieux** temps	***good old** days*

If both adjectives usually follow the noun, they are separated by **et** (*and*) or **mais** (*but*). For example:

une mer **bleue**	*a **blue** sea*
une mer **chaude**	*a **warm** sea*
une mer **chaude et bleue**	*a **warm and blue** sea*

NOTE: When there are three or more, the order depends on the tone. With Céline, you can find long extravagant sentences with multiple adjectives that are particularly striking. With Proust, comparing three or four translations of *À la recherche du temps perdu* is quite an entertaining adventure. The discrepancy in the choice of adjectives is stunning. The subtleties of feeling or of appreciation of a color may vary tremendously.

EXERCICE
3·7

Select the right adjective from the following list:

ancienne	anciennes	cher	dur	dure
forte	maigre	mince	nouvelle	tendre

1. Quand as-tu acheté ta _____ voiture?

2. Agatha n'est pas très _____. Elle ne va jamais rentrer dans cette robe.

3. Mon _____ ami, vous êtes très élégant!

4. Sophia est une _____ danseuse du Bolchoï. Elle est maintenant professeur de danse.

5. Le diplôme de journaliste est _____ à obtenir.

6. Cette viande n'est pas _____ du tout. Je vais être obligé d'en faire du ragoût.

7. Il n'a qu'un _____ salaire. Il a du mal à joindre les deux bouts.

8. Ma sœur collectionne les poupées _____.

9. Le marbre est une pierre _____.

10. La musique était vraiment trop _____. Baissez le volume!

Create a sentence by placing the words in their right order.

Example: *de grands/traversait/le train/doré/bleu/de blé/champs*

Le train bleu traversait de grands champs de blé doré.

1. grand/Antoine/un vélo/a/rouge

_____

2. des volets/la maison/pointu/verts/avait/et/petite/un toit

_____

3. un canari/rouge/avait/joli/un nez/le clown/et

_____

4. quatre/avons pêché/magnifiques/nous/truites

_____

5. roses/Sandra/ronds/et/collectionne/pailletés/les sacs

_____

6. blancs/ma chatte Myrtille/trois/et/chatons/a eu/noirs

_____

7. une cour/a/fleurie/l'école/gigantesque

_____

8. voitures/bruyantes/pleines de/encombrantes/les villes/et/polluantes/sont

_____

9. prend/minuscule/de Mathilde/des photos/nouveau/prend/l'appareil photo/belles

_____

10. exotiques/le jardin botanique/rares/et/regorge/de plantes/belles

_____

Adverbs

Adverbs are words added to a verb, an adjective, or another adverb in order to change or clarify its meaning. An adverb has no gender (masculine/feminine) or number (singular/plural).

une petite église	*a small church*
une **très** petite église	*a **very** small church*
Tu cuisines **souvent**.	*You cook **often**.*
Tu cuisines **très** bien.	*You are a **very** good cook.*
La randonnée est **trop** difficile.	*The hike is **too** difficult.*
La randonnée est **beaucoup trop** difficile.	*The hike is **far too** difficult.*

Adverbs are usually classified according to their semantic function. For example, adverbs of manner will elucidate *how* something is done, adverbs of time will tell us *when* something happened, and so on.

Adverbs of manner

admirablement	*admirably*
ainsi	*so, in this way, thus*
aussi	*also, too*
bien	*well*
comme	*as, how*
comment	*how*
debout	*standing, up*
doucement	*gently, softly*
également	*equally*
ensemble	*together*
exprès	*specially, on purpose*
gratis	*free*
gratuitement	*free*
incognito	*incognito*
lentement	*slowly*
mal	*badly, with difficulty*
mieux	*better*
plutôt	*rather, instead*
presque	*almost*
vite	*fast, quickly*
volontiers	*gladly*

Achille conduit **lentement**.	*Achille drives **slowly**.*
Le paysage est **plutôt** montagneux.	*The landscape is **rather** mountainous.*
Nous avons **presque** fini.	*We are **almost** done.*
Cela n'aurait pas dû se terminer **ainsi**.	*That should not have ended **this way**.*

Adverbs of quantity

à peine	*hardly*
à peu près	*about*
absolument	*absolutely*
à demi	*half*
assez	*enough*
aussi	*so*
autant	*as much*
autrement	*differently*
approximativement	*roughly*
beaucoup	*a lot, much*
combien	*how much*
comme	*how*
complètement	*completely*
davantage	*more*
divinement	*divinely*
drôlement	*strangely, awfully*
encore	*again, more, even*
entièrement	*completely*
environ	*about*
extrêmement	*extremely*

fort	*hard, loud, very*
grandement	*greatly*
infiniment	*infinitely*
insuffisamment	*insufficiently*
mal	*badly*
même	*even*
moins	*less*
pas mal	*not badly, rather*
passablement	*tolerably, rather*
peu	*little*
plus	*more*
plutôt	*rather*
presque	*nearly*
quasi	*almost*
quasiment	*practically*
quelque	*some, about*
si	*so*
suffisamment	*sufficiently*
tant	*so much*
tellement	*so, so much*
terriblement	*terribly, awfully*
totalement	*totally*
tout	*very, quite*
tout à fait	*quite*
très	*very*
trop	*too much*
un peu	*a little*

Tu as **à peine** mangé.	*You **hardly** ate anything.*
La maison a été **entièrement** réaménagée.	*The house was **completely** rearranged.*
Il a **tant** souffert.	*He suffered **so much**.*
Il y avait **environ** cent personnes.	*There were **about** a hundred people.*

Adverbs and adverbial phrases of time

Because there are many ways to talk about time in French, writers rely on numerous adverbs and adverbial phrases (short phrases functioning as an adverb) to achieve utmost clarity in historical narration.

actuellement	*presently*
à l'heure actuelle	*at this very moment*
alors	*then*
après	*after*
après-demain	*the day after tomorrow*
aujourd'hui	*today*
auparavant	*before*
aussitôt	*straightaway*
autrefois	*formerly*
avant	*before*
avant-hier	*the day before yesterday*
bientôt	*soon*
cependant	*however*
d'abord	*first, at first*
déjà	*already*
demain	*tomorrow*
depuis	*since, for*

désormais	*from now on*
de temps à autre	*from time to time*
de temps en temps	*from time to time*
d'habitude	*usually*
d'ordinaire	*ordinarily*
dorénavant	*from now on*
en ce moment	*at this present time*
encore	*still, again*
enfin	*at last, finally*
ensuite	*then*
hier	*yesterday*
jadis	*in times past, long ago*
longtemps	*for a long time*
maintenant	*now*
parfois	*sometimes*
puis	*then*
quelquefois	*sometimes*
rarement	*seldom*
soudain	*suddenly*
souvent	*often*
tard	*late*
tôt	*early*
toujours	*always, still*
chaque jour	*every day*
dans trois jours	*in three days (from today)*
dans une quinzaine	*in two weeks*
dans un mois	*in a month*
dans un an	*in a year*
l'avant-veille	*two days before*
la dernière semaine	*the last week (of a sequence)*
la semaine dernière	*last week*
la semaine prochaine	*next week*
la semaine suivante	*the following week*
la veille	*the day before*
le jour même	*the very day*
le lendemain	*the day after*
le surlendemain	*two days later*
tous les jours	*every day*

Autrefois, il neigeait **plus souvent**.	*It used to snow **more often**.*
Nous nous réveillons **tous les jours** à sept heures.	*We wake up **every day** at seven a.m.*
Ils ont annulé la réunion pour **le lendemain**.	*They canceled the meeting planned for **the following day**.*
Ils n'ont pas **encore** pris de décision.	*They **still** have not made a decision.*

Adverbs of location

à cet endroit	*in this place*
à côté	*next to, beside*
ailleurs	*elsewhere*
arrière	*behind*
auprès	*next to, close to*
autour	*around*
avant	*before*

ça et là	*here and there*
dedans	*inside*
dehors	*outside*
derrière	*behind*
dessous	*under*
dessus	*on top*
devant	*in front of*
ici	*here*
là	*there*
là-bas	*over there*
là-haut	*up there*
loin	*far*
où	*where*
partout	*everywhere*
près	*near, close*

Il y a des moustiques **partout**.	*There are mosquitoes **everywhere**.*
Reste **près** de moi!	*Stay **close** to me!*
Mets la valise **dessus**.	*Put the suitcase **on top**.*
Il préférerait que la réunion soit **ailleurs**.	*He'd prefer the meeting to be **elsewhere**.*

Adverbs of assertion

assurément	*most certainly*
aussi	*too*
bien	*well*
certainement	*most likely, certainly*
certes	*indeed*
d'ailleurs	*besides*
en vérité	*in fact*
oui	*yes*
précisément	*that is just the point*
si	*yes*
soit	*very well*
tout à fait	*absolutely*
volontiers	*with pleasure*
vraiment	*really*

En vérité, je suis **tout à fait** d'accord avec lui.	*In fact, I **totally** agree with him.*
Puis-je vous aider à porter ces cartons?—**Volontiers!**	*"Can I help to carry these cartons?" "**With pleasure!**"*
D'ailleurs, Bernard a toujours tort.	***Besides**, Bernard is always wrong.*
—J'aime le chocolat.—Elle **aussi**.	*"I like chocolate." "**So does she.**"*

Adverbs of negation

non	*no, not*
ne . . . rien	*not . . . anything, nothing*
ne . . . guère	*not much*
jamais	*never, not ever*
nullement	*not at all*

Nous **n'**avons **rien** dit.	*We did **not** say **anything**.*
Elle **n'**est **jamais** revenue.	*She **never** came back.*

Ils **ne** reçoivent **guère** d'argent du gouvernement.	They **hardly** get **any** money from the government.
Elle **ne** reviendra **jamais**.	She will **never** come back.

Adverbs of doubt

apparemment	*apparently*
peut-être	*maybe*
probablement	*probably*
sans doute	*probably*
toutefois	*however*
vraisemblablement	*probably*

Vraisemblablement, il va pleuvoir.	It's **probably** going to rain.
Le taxi est **peut-être** déjà arrivé.	The taxi is **maybe** already there.
Cette pièce aura **sans doute** du succès.	This play will **probably** be successful.
Peut-être viendra-t-il?	**Maybe** he will come?

EXERCICE
3·9

Complete the sentences by choosing the appropriate adverb from the following list:

admirablement	apparemment	certainement	devant	en ce moment
la semaine prochaine	nullement	près	presque	totalement

1. Tu connais cette librairie?—Oui, je passe _____ tous les jours.

2. Léna joue du violon _____.

3. Le prix de cette lampe Starck ne me semble _____ exagéré.

4. Ils viendront nous voir _____.

5. _____ il y aurait eu des fuites avant l'examen.

6. Thibaut te faisait _____ confiance.

7. Êtes-vous content de mon travail?—_____!

8. _____ les gens ne font plus confiance aux hommes politiques.

9. J'ai _____ terminé de nettoyer la cuisine.

10. La préfecture est _____ d'ici.

Position of adverbs

In compound tenses, the adverb usually follows the past participle:

Mon cerf-volant s'est envolé **très loin**.	My kite flew away **very far**.
Nous avons marché **lentement**.	We walked slowly.
Elles ont travaillé **très dur**.	They worked **very hard**.
Les Grimaud habitent **à côté**.	The Grimauds live **next door**.

With past tenses, adverbs of quantity, quality, and frequency are placed between **avoir** or **être** and the past participle:

Tu as **déjà** fini le rapport?	*You have **already** finished the report?*
Nous avons **trop** mangé.	*We ate **too much**.*
L'entreprise ne les a **pas assez** payés.	*The company did **not** pay them **enough**.*
Yanis a **mal** configuré l'ordinateur.	*Yanis has **badly** configured the computer.*

The comparisons of adjectives and adverbs

In French, comparisons of adjectives and adverbs can take three forms:

plus . . . que	*more . . . than*
moins . . . que	*less . . . than*
aussi . . . que	*as . . . as*

Vera est **plus drôle que** sa sœur.	*Vera is **funnier than** her sister.*
Mon déguisement est **moins effrayant que** le tien.	*My disguise is **less frightening than** yours.*
Cette lettre de Victor Hugo est **aussi illisible que** l'autre.	*This letter by Victor Hugo is **as illegible as** the other one.*

To compare quantities, use the following expressions:

Nous avons eu **plus** d'invités **que** l'année dernière.	*We had **more** guests **than** last year.*
Ce vieux restaurant a **moins** de clients **que** ce nouveau bistro.	*This old restaurant gets **fewer** customers **than** this new café.*
Aldo a **autant** de succès **que** Julio.	*Aldo has **as much** success **as** Julio.*

Some adjectives have irregular comparative forms:

beaucoup	*much, many*
plus	*more*
bien	*good*
mieux	*better*
bon	*good*
meilleur	*better*
mal	*bad, wrong*
pis	*worse*
mauvais	*bad*
pire	*worse*
petit	*small*
moindre	*less*

Cette sauce est **meilleure que** la mayonnaise en boîte.	*This sauce is **better than** the canned mayonnaise.*
Faustine se sent **mieux qu**'hier.	*Faustine is feeling **better than** yesterday.*
La violence urbaine est **pire qu**'il y a dix ans.	*Urban violence is **worse than** ten years ago.*
Tu as **mieux** dormi **que** la nuit dernière?	*Did you sleep **better than** last night?*

To express the ideas of *the most, the least, the best, the worst,* and so on, one uses the superlative. To form the superlative, simply add the definite article to the comparative form. Note that **de** follows the superlative where *in* is used in English:

C'est la **meilleure** chose à faire.	It's the **best** thing to do.
C'est la **pire** décision que nous ayons jamais prise.	It is the **worst** decision we ever made.
C'est la **plus haute** tour **du** monde.	It's the **highest** tower **in** the world.
C'est la **meilleure** élève **de** sa classe.	She is the **best** student **in** her class.

EXERCICE
3·10

Create a comparison sentence using the following elements:

EXAMPLE: Éloïs/Roméo/bricoleur/plus/être

Éloïs est plus bricoleur que Roméo.

1. Je/toi/colérique/moins/être

_____

2. Rachel/Coralie/maladroit/aussi/être

_____

3. Ces casques audio/performant/le plus/être

_____

4. Ce vélo en bambou/ce vélo électrique/écolo/plus/être

_____

5. Ce/le blogueur/actif/de ma région/le plus/être

_____

6. Je/prix/moindre/ce bouquet/avoir à

_____

7. Tu/Morgan/conducteur/meilleur/être

_____

8. Cet autoportrait de Gustave Courbet/magnifique/désespéré/aussi/être

_____

9. Nayla/Adrien/d'obéir/refuser/énergiquement/aussi

_____

10. Ce livre-ci/ce livre-là/mieux/se vendre

_____

Practical pronouns

4

Following a Gallic warrior: **on** and **y**

French pronouns are practical and enormously entertaining. Before we dive into this area of grammar, let me tell you about a rather enormous character from the beloved French comic-book series *Astérix*—Obélix—because his favorite expression has a place in this chapter.

This comic-book series tells humorous and erudite tales of a village in Gaul that simply refuses to become part of the Roman Empire. In this village lives Obélix, a Gaul whose idea of fun is single-handedly roughing up terrified Roman soldiers. In many episodes a Roman centurion, usually a rookie who has no idea who Obélix is, angrily commands his soldiers to charge the Gauls; Astérix (Obélix's diminutive partner in adventure for whom the series is named) looks bored; and then Obélix bellows: "**ON Y VA!**"

On y va is a frequent and versatile French expression. This phrase could be translated, depending on the context, as *Let's go there*, but what Obélix, the intrepid Gallic patriot, has in mind is closer to *Let's get up and beat those Romans into a pulp!* Because contemporary Gaul (i.e., France) is not under Roman occupation anymore, French people use this handy phrase when they want to say, *Let's go!*—because the movie will start in fifteen minutes, or because the store will close soon, or because. . . .

As you can see, this pithy phrase contains two very important pronouns, **on** and **y**. Derived from the word **homme** (as in *human being*), **on** is often translated as the English word *one*: **On ne peut pas penser à tout**, or *One cannot think of everything*. Remember that in a French sentence, **on** always occurs at the beginning of a sentence or at the beginning of an independent clause, and the following verb is always in the third-person singular. Problems appear, however, when we venture beyond basic phrases such as **Ici, on parle français** (*French is spoken here*), which is a passive-voice sentence in English. It is easy to lose one's bearings in seemingly unpredictable changes in word order. Since **on** always comes first, saying that the verb always follows does not amount to much. For example, **On ne peut pas penser à tout** is correct, but so is **On ne peut pas tout savoir**. How do we know where to put **tout** in these sentences? A good rule of thumb is that a preposition will move the **tout** to the end, while otherwise **tout** always lands between the modal verb and the infinitive.

Be careful not to take **on** sentences literally: if I wanted to have a drink with my friend Michel, I would say, **Si on prenait un verre?** This is obviously a way of saying, *Let's have a drink*. You can also use an **on** phrase to be ironic, even when targeting an individual, which would seem at odds with the general nature of **on** phrases:

Alors, **on** boit un café au lieu de travailler.

*So, **we** are drinking coffee instead of working.*

Panoramix, the venerable Druid priest in the *Astérix* story, may be partial to the letter **y**, which is also the second pronoun in Obélix's phrase, because it looks like a tree: a tree with two branches, which is significant given the dual nature of the pronoun. **Y** is related to the Latin pronoun *is* (*he*), and this is mainly amusing because the Latin *is* usually appears in conjunction with *ea* (*she*) and *id* (*it*), which gained enormous fame thanks to the efforts of Dr. Freud. Interestingly, this somewhat marginal letter, which doesn't even have a name of its own (the French call it **i grec**, or "the Greek *i*"), also serves as a quintessentially French pronoun. What makes it quintessentially French is its power to considerably lighten a phrase, to render it more concise. For example, consider the phrase:

Je vais à la pharmacie.

I am going to the pharmacy.

My friend, who needs some aspirin, is urging me to leave soon, so to reassure him, I can simply say:

J'y vais.

*I'm going (**there**).*

However, as you may have noticed, French speakers also use **y** in a different way: namely, to refer to thoughts and ideas. For example:

Barbara pense à sa thèse de troisième cycle.

Barbara is thinking about her graduate thesis.

We can considerably shorten that phrase by saying:

Barbara **y** pense.

*Barbara is thinking **about it**.*

But, you may protest, Barbara's thesis is still an abstraction, it is not a place in the physical universe.

Well, according to the logic of the French language, Barbara's thesis, or anything anyone can think about, *is* a point in a universe that includes both the physical world and a person's mental universe. French likes to be comprehensive. Also, remember that **y** likes the company of the preposition **à**.

And especially in conversation, when you are asked a question like:

Pensez-vous à votre avenir en Australie avec votre mari et vos enfants?

Are you thinking about your future in Australia with your husband and your children?

you could, of course, answer:

Oui, je pense à mon avenir en Australie avec mon mari et mes enfants.

But it would be too long, and it would sound silly. There is a chance the person who asked the question would already be gone before you finished your sentence. Just say: **J'y pense**. Here are some other examples:

Je pense à son nouveau projet.	*I am thinking about his new project.*
J'y pense.	*I am thinking **about it**.*
Louise s'intéresse à la biologie.	*Louise is interested in biology.*
Louise s'**y** intéresse.	*Louise is interested **in it**.*

Fine, you say, but how do we explain the following?

Sarah parle de son travail.	*Sarah is talking about her work.*
Sarah **en** parle.	*Sarah is talking **about it**.*

What happened to **y**? Well, **y** stayed at home, because it does not consort with the preposition **de**. In the grand French dichotomy of "**de** verbs" and "**à** verbs," **y** is in the "**à** camp," which is why **en** must report for duty when Sarah is talking about her work. Always pay attention to the preposition!

Before you get too comfortable with **y** and **en**, you must know that these two pronouns should not be used for persons. In other words, despite their adventuresome spirit, they avoid the territory of personal pronouns. So Manon may not use **y** or **en** when she is thinking (or talking) about her mother. In this case, the good old personal pronoun hastens to assert its rights:

Manon parle de sa mère.	*Manon is talking about her mother.*
Manon parle **d'elle**.	*Manon is talking **about her**.*
Manon pense à sa mère.	*Manon is thinking about her mother.*
Manon pense **à elle**.	*Manon is thinking **about her**.*

Of course, there are some exceptions. When you want to be ironic about someone or when the people mentioned are not specific, **en** can be used.

Surtout ne me parle pas de ton amie Jeanne!	*Please don't talk to me about your friend Jeanne!*
Surtout ne m'**en** parle pas!	*Please don't talk to me **about her**!*

Here it is obvious Jeanne is not on the speaker's list of favorite people.

Avez-vous des amis à Lyon?	*Do you have friends in Lyon?*
Oui, j'**en** ai.	*Yes, I do. / Yes, I have some.*

Here **en** is acceptable since the friends are not identified. They remain vague entities.

In the meantime, let's return to our Gallic friends. Astérix, who is not in a particularly belligerent mood, decides to flex his grammatical muscle. So turning to his huge friend, he says:

Vas-**y**!	*Go ahead!*

Thanks to the diminutive Gallic warrior, we know that in an imperative phrase, **y** always scurries to the end of the phrase.

Would you like to start a sentence with **y**? Obélix often does, particularly when he's looking for Roman soldiers:

Trouvera-t-on des Romains dans la forêt?	*Will we find some Romans in the forest?*
Y trouvera-t-on des Romains?	*Will we find some Romans **there**?*

No doubt, you have used the following handy French construction:

Il **y** a . . .	*There is . . .*

If you share Obélix's insatiable curiosity, you may ask your friend:

Y a-t-il une librairie française dans ton quartier?	*Is **there** a French bookstore in your neighborhood?*

*Re-create each sentence, replacing the words in boldface by **y**.*

1. Enzo compte devenir avocat **à Dijon**.

_____

2. Lucas va **à la piscine** cet après-midi.

_____

3. Lina prête attention à **ce qui se passe autour d'elle**.

_____

4. N'entrez pas **dans le cabinet de travail de Julia**!

_____

5. Va **chez Louis**!

_____

6. Pourquoi n'avez-vous pas répondu **à ma lettre**?

_____

7. Jade ne croit pas **à la théorie de la relativité**.

_____

8. Hugo tient **à sa carrière diplomatique**.

_____

9. Mon cousin s'accroche **à toutes ses illusions**.

_____

10. Je m'intéresse **à l'histoire de France**.

_____

The magic potion: en

Before every battle with the Romans, Astérix and his comrades line up for a dose of the chief Druid's magic potion, which bestows temporary superhuman strength on a warrior. Obélix, who fell into the magician's cauldron when he was little, feels left out because he doesn't need any:

    Je n'**en** ai pas besoin.   *I don't need **any**.*

As you can imagine, the centurion's misguided order to arrest the two comedians falls on deaf ears, for every single soldier in that Roman century knows about the magic potion. Sure enough, Obélix is quick to react to the centurion's foolishness, but his response astounds everybody, for he simply bellows: "**Va-t-en!**" As you are struggling to understand Obélix's behavior, it occurs to you that the Gallic giant used the pronoun **en** to say *Go away!* Impressive, isn't it? Obélix has just shown us the pronominal verb **s'en aller** (never to be confused with **aller**) in action!

The ever-practical pronoun can also replace a noun that follows a partitive article. If this sounds too technical, imagine the aftermath of a successful wild boar hunt in Obélix's beloved forest. At the magnificent feast honoring yet another Roman military fiasco, Astérix is offering his friend some roast boar:

Veux-tu du sanglier rôti?	*Would you like some roast boar?*
En veux-tu?	*Would you like **some**?*

How would you answer the preceding question?

J'**en** veux bien.	*Yes, I would like **some**.*

No need to be disoriented by the moving pronoun: in both cases, it directly precedes the verb, which is in the driver's seat. Since we already know that the preposition **en** favors verbal and adjectival constructions that contain the preposition **de**, we will not be surprised by the following phrases:

Bill Gates a beaucoup d'argent.	*Bill Gates has a lot of money.*
Bill Gates **en** a beaucoup.	*Bill Gates has a lot (**of it**).*

Finally, remember that **en** is handy when the object of a phrase is somewhat undefined. Note the indefinite article in:

J'ai une voiture.	*I have a car.*
J'**en** ai une.	*I have one.*

The pronoun **en** fits right in.

When the object is well-defined, there is no room for **en**:

Tu as ton dictionnaire?	*Do you have your dictionary?*
Tu l'as?	*Do you have it?*
Je l'ai.	*I have it.*

With pronominal verbs, if the indirect pronoun is a person, the disjunctive pronouns (**moi, toi, (lui, elle soi, nous, vous, eux, elles**) must be used. Compare:

Simone a peur des souris.	Simone **en** a peur.
Il veut une nouvelle armoire.	Il **en** veut une.
Nous commandons trois livres.	Nous **en** commandons trois.
Elle se souvient de son adresse.	Elle s'**en** souvient.
Hélène parle de son voyage à Bali.	Hélène **en** parle.
Hélène parle du commandant de bord.	Hélène parle **de lui**.
Sylvia s'est approchée de la rivière.	Sylvia s'**en** est approchée.
Sylvia s'est approchée du marchand de légumes.	Sylvia s'est approché **de lui**.

With the indirect object **en**, the past participle never agrees in the past tenses. Compare:

Elle a envoyé la chemise blanche qu'il voulait.	Elle **la** lui a envoyé**e**.
Elle lui a envoyé une chemise blanche.	Elle lui **en** a envoyé une.

It is important to acquire the reflex: direct or indirect? Things or people? Regular or pronominal verbs? That will help you sort out all these pronouns.

*Re-create the sentences, replacing the words in boldface by the pronoun **en**.*

1. Nous avons besoin d'un directeur qui soit capable **de gérer une entreprise.**

   _____

2. Les employés de notre bureau se plaignent **du nouveau règlement.**

   _____

3. Anne se chargera **de l'éducation de ses deux filles.**

   _____

4. Lucas ne se souvient pas **de ses années de lycée.**

   _____

5. Natalie Dessay, qui est une grande chanteuse, jouera aussi **du piano** ce soir.

   _____

6. Un bon conseil: ne te mêle pas **de leur vie.**

   _____

7. Si on licencie son assistant, Adam sera mécontent **de la situation.**

   _____

8. J'aimerais bien accompagner Martin à la réception à l'ambassade du Luxembourg, mais je n'ai pas **de robe de soirée.**

   _____

9. Bien qu'elle les trouve de plus en plus envahissantes, Lilou s'occupe **de ses plantes** avec minutie.

   _____

10. Malgré les critiques de certains de ses collègues, Mme Bréval est fière **des fiches pédagogiques qu'elle a créées.**

    _____

Direct object pronouns

As you know, English has the following direct object pronouns: *me, you, him/her/it, us, you* (plural), *them*. The French equivalents are quite straightforward, except for the two forms of the object pronoun *you*: the informal **te** and the formal **vous**, which is also the plural form of *you*, as in *You children really need to put on your shoes.*

NOTE: Always be aware of the difference between **te** and **vous** in everyday speech, for mistakes can be quite embarrassing. This is where grammar works to help us avoid a social faux pas. If you're telling your fellow student that you see her or him, **Je te vois** works quite well. However, if you're talking to the professor, imagine, if you will, that you're seeing double: Who is standing next to Mme Bréval? Her sister? Blissfully unaware of your mental gymnastics, Mme Bréval will be quite pleased to hear you say, **Je vous vois**. Don't be too discouraged by formal address in French: you will never fail if you remember the "seeing double rule." Take heart: compared to Italian or German, formal address in French is a breeze. But let's continue our investigation of direct object pronouns.

When it comes to the use of direct object pronouns, French is more inclusive than English: **le**, **la**, and **les** can refer to people, animals, and things, which means that they can refer to anything. Let's imagine a few questions to which **je l'aime** (note the elision before a word starting with a vowel) would be a suitable answer: **Aimez-vous Caroline? Aimez-vous votre labrador? Aimez-vous la littérature française?**

Strange as it may seem, the most challenging aspect of this particular grammatical category is word order. By and large, French, just like English, is an SVO (subject-verb-object) language, which means that the SVO sequence is its natural order. Natural, indeed, but since Nature likes to play games, we must be prepared for surprises. Remember: **On ne peut pas tout savoir!**

Wishing to assert themselves, so to speak, direct object pronouns replace the "natural" SVO order with an SOV (subject-object-verb) sequence. For example, when I want to rephrase the sentence **J'aime Caroline** as a direct object pronoun phrase, I may not say **J'aime la**, which would be a literal translation of the English *I love her*. I must say **Je l'aime**.

While the SOV sequence remains unchanged in negative sentences, problems may arise if we misplace the negative particle **ne**. One should always keep an eye on the negative particle in French, since it seems to have a mind of its own. For example, under normal circumstances, the negative particle always precedes the verb: **Je n'aime pas les maths**. However, in an SOV phrase, and this would include any sentence containing a direct object pronoun, the negative particle must, strange as it seems, directly precede the object: **Je ne les aime pas**. The negative particle still precedes the verb, but the direct object pronoun manages to elbow its way in.

If you find the SOV sequence strange, interrogative sentences might throw you for a loop, because they literally reverse the SVO order. Returning to Mme Bréval's classroom, we may, in an effort to reassure a student who thinks that the teacher is invisible, ask if he or she sees Mme Bréval. Just to make things a bit more challenging, we will, instead of asking literally **Voyez-vous Mme Bréval?**, use the appropriate direct object pronoun. Figuring out the correct pronoun (**la**) may be easy, but word order poses a problem. The direct object pronoun "insists" on leading the sentence, which means that the word order, in this case, is OVS, the reverse of SVO. In other words, **La Voyez-vous?** Startled by the strange word sequence, the student has no choice but to return to reality and admit that the Invisible French Teacher is just another urban myth.

The case interlude

Before we proceed, a few words about cases, which still haunt some modern languages, including English and French. This has nothing to do with criminal cases, although there is a gambling connection, since the word *case* comes from the Latin (of course!) *casus*, which means *fall* and happens when a die is cast. Greek grammarians, who obviously liked the gambling metaphor, thought nothing of deriving a fundamental grammatical term from dice.

So in the old days, when Latin was a modern language, not only verbs but also nouns (as well as pronouns) had individual endings. In fact, in inflected languages (one is almost tempted to say *infected*), a case is akin to a garment that a noun is not allowed to shed. No nudist beaches for nouns! Far from being the invention of an evil genie who hates students, cases alert the reader to the particular function a noun performs in a sentence. For example, the **nominative case** identifies, or *names*, a particular noun as the subject of a sentence.

Although English and French nouns (fortunately) lack case endings, ordinary English sentences can show us the concept of case. For example, in the sentence *John loves Mary*, the subject, John, is in the nominative case. As the direct object, Mary is in the *accusative case*, which tells us that a noun is the object of an action.

Believe it or not, there is an English pronoun that sometimes takes a case ending! Granted, this ending is on its way out, but it's still in use. Indeed, modern usage accepts this phrase, "Who did you call?" But I bet Miss Manners would say that the *correct* phrase is "*Whom* did you call?" Well, that *-m*, which we may choose to ignore, is a genuine case ending, telling us that the pronoun *who*, in this particular instance, is in the accusative case. In English, *-m* is also a dative case ending, as evidenced by the archaic but still used phrase *To Whom It May Concern*.

The *genitive case* implies a relationship. For example, instead of saying *John's brother*, we could use the form that English grammarians have baptized "the Norman genitive." For example, the Norman genitive *brother of John* corresponds, in fact, to **le frère de Jean**. Unlike Latin, where a genitive ending would be tacked onto the noun *John*, French, as indicated by the Norman genitive, uses a preposition as a case marker.

In the same vein, the preposition *to* may be used to identify a noun in the *dative case*. The dative is the emotional "giving" case: "Write me a letter!" Note the emotional difference between the warmth of "Tell me a story" and the somewhat formal "Enlighten me!" Understanding and internalizing the distinction between the dative (the indirect object case) and the accusative (the direct object case) will stand you in good stead whenever you're unsure about French pronouns. You don't have to learn any case endings; you're safe—Latin can't get you! An intuitive grasp of the four cases occurring in French is all you need.

Accusative case

At this point, it would be good to review the *accusative case*, because a direct object is always in the accusative case: *John loves Mary*. In a regular SVO phrase, the object, to state the obvious, is at the end. The important point to remember here is the following: both the object and the pronoun acting as its substitute stay close to the verb.

Yo-Yo Ma joue le Concerto pour violoncelle en la mineur de Saint-Saëns.	*Yo-Yo Ma plays the Cello Concerto in A minor by Saint-Saëns.*
Yo-Yo Ma **le** joue.	*Yo-Yo Ma plays **it**.*

The following is probably not a factual statement, but let us use it anyway:

Yo-Yo Ma ne joue pas le Concerto pour violoncelle en ré majeur de Haydn.	*Yo-Yo May does not play the Cello Concerto in D major by Haydn.*
Yo-Yo Ma ne **le** joue pas.	*Yo-Yo Ma does not play **it**.*

What happens when a direct object is replaced by a direct object pronoun in a phrase?

Il joue le concerto.	*He plays the concerto.*
Il **le** joue.	*He plays **it**.*

If you compare the two preceding sentences, you will notice that the verb and the object have switched places. The object precedes the verb. Remember this little maneuver, for it will come in handy when you run into interrogative sentences. For example, here's the title of a famous novel by Françoise Sagan:

Aimez-vous Brahms?	*Do you like Brahms?*

What if the famous novelist had wanted to use the direct object pronoun?

L'aimez-vous?	*Do you like **him**?*

Incidentally, a phrase such as **Je l'aime** says nothing about the direct object's gender. Despite this particular ambivalence, verb-object agreement is a rule that always remains in force. For example:

Yo-Yo Ma joue **le** concerto de Schumann	*Yo-Yo Ma plays the concerto by Schumann.*
Yo-Yo Ma **le** joue.	*Yo-Yo Ma plays it.*
Yo-Yo Ma joue **la** deuxième sonate de Beethoven.	*Yo-Yo Ma plays the second sonata by Beethoven.*
Yo-Yo Ma **la** joue.	*Yo-Yo Ma plays it.*
Janina Fialkowska joue **les** trois sonates de Chopin.	*Janina Fialkowska plays the three sonatas by Chopin.*
Janina Fialkowksa **les** joue.	*Janina Fialkowska plays **them**.*

We should not be surprised by the subject-verb inversion in a sentence. Inversion enables us to ask questions. A phrase like **L'aimez-vous** may look strange at first glance, but since the pronoun precedes the verb, it has nowhere else to go when the verb occupies the second slot in the sentence.

Finally, the direct object, as well as its pronoun, appears at the end of an imperative phrase. Seen by the naked eye as a verb-object structure, the sequence seems quite natural, since it is the verb that expresses the command. Consequently, the pronoun has no other alternative but to go to the end of the phrase.

Pianist Martha Argerich and violinist Anne-Sophie Mutter want to play Beethoven's "Archduke" trio, but Yo-Yo Ma is nowhere to be found. In this situation, the natural thing to say is:

Appelez **Yo-Yo**!	Appelez-**le**!

However, if the two musicians suddenly decide to go home, they will say:

N'appelez pas **Yo-Yo**!	Ne **l'**appelez pas!

In a negative imperative phrase, the pronoun precedes the verb.

Emphatic interlude

In an affirmative imperative phrase, first- and second-personal singular direct object pronouns (**me** and **te**) don't work, because a phrase such as **Invitez-*me*** sounds anemic, as well as ungrammatical, in French. This is where *emphatic*, or disjunctive, pronouns come to the rescue. *Emphatic* is self-explanatory; the term *disjunctive* may seem cryptic. It is supposed to mean "out of place," which probably sounds too ordinary to a grammarian's ear.

Here's an example:

Mes amis adorent le café, mais **moi**, je ne bois que du thé!	*My friends adore coffee, but as for **me**, I drink only tea.*

Despite the popularity of *disjunctive*, it is better to stick to the term *emphatic*, for it really captures the essence of this particular proposition. For example, King Louis XIV could have said:

Je suis l'État.	*I am the State.*

However, feeling strongly about the issue, he declared:

L'État, c'est **moi**.	*It is I who am the State. (The State is me.)*

In France, when a person wants to know who is at the door, the correct answer, if we assume that the caller's voice has been recognized, is not **je** (which is semantically correct, but otherwise either comical or all wrong) but **moi**. We all know (thanks again, Dr. Freud) that the Latin word *ego*, the ancestor, believe it or not, of the French **je**, means *I*. But just as in Latin and in English (note the difference between *I am your teacher* and *You teach **me***), in emotionally charged phrases the concept of *I* leaves the nominative case and settles in the dative or accusative realm. Why does this happen? Because the genius of language makes a clear distinction between affirmative, declarative, or factual (*I am your teacher*) statements and emotionally charged (*You teach me*) statements. You can almost feel the tension in a phrase like:

Appelle-**moi**!   *Call **me**!*
Donne-**moi** ta main!   *Give **me** your hand!*

You have no doubt heard children use the ungrammatical construction *Give me* [indirect object: dative] *it* [direct object: accusative] instead of the correct form *Give it to me*. English syntax places the direct object first, but the ungrammatical child favors the indirect object, because in this case the indirect object is the child's own ego. Incidentally, the third case is named the *dative*, which is related to the word *data* (i.e., things that are given) because of the strong emotional charge of the verb *to give*.

Back to direct object pronouns

As we already know, the pronoun stays close to the verb. In compound tenses, such as the omnipresent **passé composé**, the pronoun will precede the auxiliary verb.

Le claveciniste a joué quelques morceaux   *The harpsichordist played a few pieces*
   de François Couperin.   *by François Couperin.*
Il **les** a joués.   *He played **them**.*

Did the past participle startle you? Of course not!

EXERCICE

4·3

Re-create the sentences, replacing the words in boldface by the direct object pronoun.

1. Léo a choisi **le sujet pour sa thèse de doctorat.**

   _____

2. Jade a obtenu **son diplôme en sociologie** l'année dernière.

   _____

3. Emma a publié **le meilleur essai sur la pensée chinoise.**

   _____

4. N'oubliez pas de consulter **votre médecin**!

   _____

5. N'acceptez pas **les résultats d'un sondage mal conçu.**

   _____

6. As-tu vu **le nouveau film de Pedro Almodovar?**

   _____

7. J'ai finalement compris **sa décision.**

   _____

8. Si tu arrives à Paris avant la fin du mois, appelle **mon ami Yanis**.

_____

9. Je soutiens **la candidature de mon ami Érik à la présidence de la République**.

_____

10. Rendez **l'ordinateur portable** à Juliette!

_____

Indirect object pronouns

As you may have guessed, emphatic pronouns are used for the first- and second-person singular:

> Envoyez-**moi** le manuscrit de son
> nouveau roman!

> *Send me the manuscript of his*
> *new novel!*

This is what direct object and indirect object pronouns have in common. Where they differ is in the third person (singular and plural):

> Donne-**lui** son cahier vert!
> Apportez-**leur** les documents qui se
> trouvent dans le tiroir!

> *Give **him** his green notebook!*
> *Bring **them** the documents that are*
> *in the drawer!*

Don't forget: think of the verb *to give* and review the dative case when you're dealing with the indirect object.

Finally, a rule that may seem strange: the third person (singular and plural) works for both genders:

> Ne **lui** donnez rien!

> *Don't give **him** (or **her**) anything!*

This will seem less strange when you remember that the pronoun is a versatile animal. For example, the pronoun **je** represents both genders, and so do many others.

EXERCICE

4·4

Re-create the sentences, replacing the words in boldface by the indirect object pronoun.

1. Tom a fait un joli cadeau **à la sœur de son collègue du bureau**.

_____

2. Valérie a raconté de belles histoires aux **petits-enfants**.

_____

3. Hugo, qui vient de choisir la carrière de magicien, annoncera sa décision **à ses parents** demain.

_____

4. Mme Bréval a expliqué le subjonctif **aux étudiants de M. Indicat**.

   _____

5. Le petit archipel que nous voyons à l'horizon appartient **à mon amie Lola**.

   _____

6. Au risque de l'offusquer, Léna n'a pas donné son numéro de téléphone **à Mathis**.

   _____

7. La classe de traduction a offert un carré Hermès **à Mme Bréval**.

   _____

8. Félix est un chien très paresseux, mais il apporte _Le Monde_ **à Maylis**.

   _____

9. À la différence de son ami Valentin, qui est apolitique, Antoine aime envoyer des analyses de la situation politique **au rédacteur en chef du Figaro**.

   _____

10. Ne dites rien **à Lina**, car elle a beaucoup de soucis à cause de sa voisine.

    _____

What comes first? The order of object pronouns in a phrase

If you remember the kid who said _Give me it,_ you will know what to do. For in a sentence containing both types of pronouns (direct and indirect object), the indirect object pronoun usually comes first.

Elle **te** donne le livre.	_She gives **you** the book._
Elle **te le** donne.	_She gives **it** to **you**._

Unfortunately, this rule does not work for the third person (singular and plural). There is a switch—the direct object pronoun comes first:

Elle **lui** donne le livre.	_She gives **him** the book._
Elle **le lui** donne.	_She gives **it** to **him**._

Random as this switch may seem, it is not. The first and second persons denote a world of closeness, intimacy, and emotional intensity. After all, the first and second persons (_you_ and _I_) constitute a relationship, establishing a fundamental duality. In fact, in French, the third person singular pronoun, **il/elle,** stems from the Latin _ille/illa,_ one of the four pronouns that, depending on the context, may act as the third person singular pronoun in Latin. It should be pointed out that these Latin pronouns are all demonstrative. In other words, Latin does not have a personal pronoun for the third person, which may explain a certain inherited ambivalence in French about the third person. We can illustrate this ambivalence by rephrasing Louis the XIV's grandiose dictum as a reported statement:

L'État, c'est **lui**.	*It is **he** who is the State.*

This is a different statement: somewhat colorless and distant, devoid of any emotional intensity. When I say:

Elle **me le** donne.	*She gives **it** to **me**.*

the indirect pronoun **me** comes first, because it is all about *me*. And since I know that I'm getting something (a gift?), the object, because it is overshadowed by the emotionally engaged imperfect subject, stays in second place. However, everything changes once we move on to the third person: not being *me*, the indirect object nonchalantly "allows" the direct object to take the initial spot:

Elle **le lui** donne.	*She gives **it** to **him/her**.*

EXERCICE
4·5

Re-create the sentences, replacing the words in boldface by the appropriate pronoun.

1. Inès a envoyé **le corrigé de son essai à Mme Leroux.**

_____

2. Fahed a recommandé **son restaurant favori à ses collègues de bureau.**

_____

3. Ambre donne **des conseils aux nouveaux professeurs.**

_____

4. Le médecin a prescrit **de nouveaux exercices de physiothérapie à mon frère.**

_____

5. Ethan a raconté **des mensonges à son psychanalyste.**

_____

6. Arthur a envoyé **sa nouvelle symphonie à un chef d'orchestre parisien.**

_____

7. Hugo dédiera **son premier roman policier à sa femme.**

_____

8. Aujourd'hui, je vais demander **une augmentation de salaire au patron.**

_____

9. J'offrirai **un iPod à ma nièce** car elle s'est occupée du jardin.

_____

10. Sans pouvoir justifier la raison, Louis veut emprunter **une somme importante à la banque.**

_____

Relative pronouns

Relative pronouns enable us to avoid repeating a subject from a previous clause. For example, if relative pronouns didn't exist, we would have to make do with awkward two-sentence constructions such as:

I know a girl named Barbara. Barbara attends our local university.

Thanks to relative pronouns, we can say:

*I know a girl named Barbara, **who** attends our local university.*

These pronouns are called *relative* because they establish a clear *relation* between two clauses. A person who hears the entire phrase knows, without thinking, that the word *who* in the subordinate clause refers to the subject or object of the main clause. In this particular main clause, Barbara is the object, but we can also say:

*Barbara, **who** attends our local university, likes geometry.*

Here Barbara is the subject, and interestingly, the subordinate clause inserts itself into the middle of the main clause. Either way, the relative pronoun faithfully performs its duties.

The **qui/que** conundrum

As you may have noticed, French relative pronouns have a particular way of confusing the poor learner.

For example, the minute we assume that **qui** refers to persons only, it jumps off that bandwagon and starts consorting with things, objects, concepts, and anything that is not a person. So if **qui** and **que** refer to *everything*, how do we tell them apart? Indeed, they both replace nouns, but **qui** replaces a *subject* (nominative case), while **que** takes the spot of an *object* (accusative case). Yet if you want to tell someone how irritated you are by your friend's desire to always be right, you may be fooled into saying:

Ce que m'énerve est son désir d'avoir toujours raison.

It almost sounds right, but it's not, because the pronoun **que** is masquerading as a subject, which is against the rules. The sentence is saying, what bugs me is my friend's obsession with always being right, which means that I am bugged *by* his obsession—I am affected by something. In other words, since *I* is the object, the annoying obsession can only be the subject. Consequently, what *I* must say is:

Ce **qui** m'énerve est son désir d'avoir toujours raison.	*What annoys me is his desire to always be right.*

Note that in similar phrases, the verb **penser** occurs in conjunction with the pronoun **que**. Why? Because, as a thinking *subject*, I am the active force that affects or modifies the content of my thoughts: what I think about is the *object* of my mental activity. For example:

Ce **que** je pense de Victor n'a aucune importance.	*What I think of Victor is unimportant.*

In fact, if we expand the previous phrase, we will have *both* forms of this particular pronoun in a single sentence:

Ce **que** je pense de Victor, **qui** m'agace, est sans importance.	*What I think of Victor, **who** annoys me, is unimportant.*

Here are some examples to illustrate the difference between **qui** and **que**:

Nous félicitons le musicien **qui** a composé cette belle sonate.

*We congratulate the musician **who** composed this beautiful sonata.*

Fabien a répondu à toutes les questions de grammaire **que** Mme Bréval lui avait posées.

*Fabian has answered all the grammar questions **that** Mme Bréval had asked him.*

Marianne est une journaliste **que** ses collègues admirent.

*Marianne is a journalist **whom/that** her colleagues admire.*

Nathan fait partie d'un groupe **qui** soutient la justice sociale.

*Nathan belongs to a group **that** supports social justice.*

Simone travaille pour une entreprise **qui** encourage l'esprit d'invention.

*Simone works for a company **that** encourages inventiveness.*

**EXERCICE
4·6**

*Complete the sentences by inserting either **qui** or **que**.*

1. Fais quelque chose _____ te fera plaisir.

2. Rossini a composé plusieurs opéras _____ le public adore.

3. Mme Lemaire est un professeur _____ Louise aime bien.

4. Ethan me dit que la grammaire française est une matière _____ l'intéresse.

5. *Bouvard et Pécuchet* est un roman _____ j'aime lire et relire.

6. *Le Bon usage* de Grevisse et Goosse est une grammaire _____ sera utile pour les étudiants.

7. Le tableau _____ je veux te vendre se trouve dans mon atelier.

8. Le tableau _____ était dans mon atelier a été vendu.

9. Le garçon _____ Zoé considère comme brillant et sophistiqué s'appelle Jacob.

10. Le garçon _____ considère Zoé comme brillante et sophistiquée s'appelle Arthur.

What's the deal with **dont**?

Everybody knows this handy French word that invariably turns into *don't* when we forget to keep our spell-checker in check. Interestingly, **dont** is a pronoun that replaces pronouns, especially those of the cumbersome variety—for example, **duquel**, **de laquelle**, **desquels**, and **desquelles**. For example, the sentence:

Le bibliothécaire **duquel** je me souviens travaille à la Bibliothèque Nationale.

*The librarian **whom** I remember works at the National Library.*

is considerably improved when we rephrase it as:

Le bibliothécaire **dont** je me souviens travaille à la Bibliothèque nationale.

The preposition (always look for the preposition!) that usually directs us to **dont** is **de**, which, as you know, appears in conjunction with particular verbs and expressions.

Jean a besoin **de** ses manuels de grammaire.   *Jean needs his grammar textbooks.*

This would be a good time to review constructions such as **avoir besoin de**, **se servir de**, **souffrir de**, **se souvenir de**, **décider de**, **s'enivrer de**, **hériter de**, **manquer de**, **oublier de**, **repentir de**, **triompher de**, and so on.

J'ai besoin **des** autres.   *I need (other) people.*
Voici les gens **dont** j'ai besoin.   *Here are the people **whom** I need.*

Finally, true to its versatile spirit, **dont** also expresses possession.

Jacques connaît des philosophes **dont** les meilleurs amis sont sociologues.   *Jacques knows philosophers **whose** best friends are sociologists.*

EXERCICE 4·7

Complete the following sentences.

1. Balzac est un romancier _____ les romans sont lus dans le monde entier.

2. Le manuel de grammaire _____ les étudiants se servent est bilingue.

3. La tablette numérique _____ Sophie a besoin est assez chère.

4. Le camarade de lycée _____ tu parles est ministre dans le gouvernement actuel.

5. Les étudiants _____ le professeur vient de recevoir le Prix Nobel sont tous d'excellents scientifiques.

6. J'habite dans une ville _____ le transport public est dans un très mauvais état.

7. Nous nous sommes perdus dans un vieux quartier _____ l'aspect extérieur avait beaucoup changé.

8. Clara est allée voir un spectacle _____ tous les billets ont été rapidement vendus.

9. Avez-vous essayé le vin rouge _____ notre petit village est très fier?

10. Notre université vient d'engager plusieurs professeurs _____ certains manquent de qualifications.

You say **ce qui**, I say **ce que**, they say **ce dont**...

Frustrated by a boring novel, I can say, *I find boring novels annoying.* Of course, if I want to be a little more emphatic, I can exclaim, *What I find annoying are boring novels!*

You can do the same thing in French. In fact, we have already used this type of phrase in our discussion of the **qui/que** conundrum. A tiny demonstrative pronoun, **ce** is an enormously productive particle, since it can be used to create a huge variety of sentences. Interestingly, **ce** works quite well in tandem with several relative pronouns.

Ce qui figures as the subject of a dependent (subordinate) clause:

Je ne sais pas **ce qui** a provoqué leur colère.	*I don't know **what** provoked their anger.*
Ce qui m'intéresse, c'est cette nouvelle par Michel Tournier.	***What** interests me is this short story by Michel Tournier.*

Ce que figures as the direct object of a dependent clause:

Je comprends **ce que** tu es en train de faire.	*I understand **what** you are doing.*
Ce que tu dis est absurde.	***What** you are saying is absurd.*

Ce dont is used in phrases containing verbs that go with the preposition **de**:

Il a besoin **de** quelque chose; elle ne sait pas **ce dont** il a besoin.	*He needs something; she does not know **what** he needs.*

Ce à quoi is used in phrases containing verbs that go with the preposition **à**:

Mme Joliot voudrait savoir **(ce) à quoi** sa fille aspire.	*Madame Joliot would like to know **what** her daughter is aspiring to.*
Ce à quoi l'entreprise s'intéresse, c'est à la création d'une crèche.	*What the company is interested in is creating a day care center.*

You may have noticed that these combined pronouns, which have neither gender nor number and generally refer to concepts and ideas, work really well in phrases describing an uncertain situation or state of affairs.

EXERCICE

4·8

Complete the following sentences with the discussed compound pronouns.

1. _____ Jean-Claude parle est très bizarre.

2. _____ Emmanuelle s'intéresse, c'est à la musique de Jean-Sébastien Bach.

3. _____ je décris dans mon roman, c'est la rivalité entre deux familles puissantes.

4. _____ est passionnant dans son récit, c'est son évocation de la vie parisienne à la fin de l'Ancien Régime.

5. _____ je ne comprends pas, c'est son manque d'enthousiasme.

6. _____ Charles se souvient, c'est de sa jeunesse en Italie.

7. _____ s'est passé hier dans la capitale, c'est un défi pour le gouvernement.

8. _____ Dominique a besoin, c'est de votre aide financière.

9. _____ mes parents aiment, c'est un bon polar de Georges Simenon.

10. _____ tu as envie dépasse notre budget.

Where are you going, when are you going?

Inquiries pertaining to a person's destination or location contain the multipurpose pronoun **où**, which may also replace **dans lequel**, **sur lequel**, and **par lequel**.

> Villefranche-de-Panat, le village **où** mon ami Patrice habite, est près de Rodez.
> *Villefranche-de-Panat, the village **where** my friend Patrice lives, is near Rodez.*

In the sentence above, **où** replaces **dans lequel**, making the phrase more elegant.

We could say that **où** "believes" in the idea of a time-space continuum, for it also refers to a point in time. For example:

> Le jour **où** il fera beau, nous ferons une promenade avec ton amie Martine.
> *On the day **when** the weather is nice, we will go for a walk with your friend Martine.*

Quite a vague "point," you might say, but **où** isn't very picky. Naturally, it can also refer to a precise point:

> Il pleuvait le jour **où** tu es né.
> *It rained on the day you were born.*

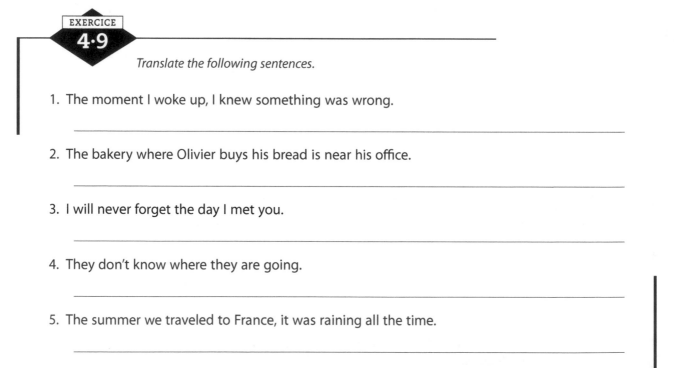

EXERCICE
4·9

Translate the following sentences.

1. The moment I woke up, I knew something was wrong.

   _____

2. The bakery where Olivier buys his bread is near his office.

   _____

3. I will never forget the day I met you.

   _____

4. They don't know where they are going.

   _____

5. The summer we traveled to France, it was raining all the time.

   _____

The past tenses

The immediate past tense

Just as **aller** (*to go*) combined with the infinitive expresses an action that is going to happen, **venir** (*to come*) in the present tense + **de**, combined with a verb in the infinitive, expresses an action that has just taken place. Although **venir** is in the present tense in French, it conveys an idea in the past in English:

venir	to come
je viens	*I come*
tu viens	*you come*
il/elle vient	*he/she comes*
nous venons	*we come*
vous venez	*you come*
ils/elles viennent	*they come*

Arnaud **vient de brûler** le gigot.	*Arnaud **just burnt** the leg of lamb.*
Vous **venez de commencer** des études de médecine.	*You **have just started** to study medicine.*
Je **viens de faire** une réservation chez Henri.	*I **just made** a reservation at Henri's.*
Nous **venons de nous inscrire** à un cours de français.	*We **just signed up** for a French class.*

The **passé composé**

Several tenses can be used to describe past events in French. The most common is the **passé composé**, also called the *compound past*, or the perfect tense. It expresses a single past action that has been completed. It is composed of two parts: an auxiliary verb, **avoir** or **être**, and a past participle. Most verbs form their **passé composé** with **avoir**. The past participle is formed by adding an ending to the verb stem.

Regular past participles take the following endings:

-er verbs → **é**	**donner** (*to give*)	**donné** (*given*)
-ir verbs → **i**	**sentir** (*to smell*)	**senti** (*smelled*)
-re verbs → **u**	**perdre** (*to lose*)	**perdu** (*lost*)

NOTE: The **passé composé** can be translated in different ways in English. Its English equivalent depends on the context:

	I lost my glasses.
J'ai perdu mes lunettes.	*I have lost my glasses.*
	I did lose my glasses.

As in the present tense, there are three ways to make a question:

Vous avez visité l'abbaye?	*You visited the abbey?*
Avez-vous visité l'abbaye?	*Did you visit the abbey?*
Est-ce que vous avez visité l'abbaye?	*Did you visit the abbey?*

In the negative form, the **ne** (**n'**) is placed in front of **avoir** or **être** and the **pas** after **avoir** or **être**:

Tu **as écrit** au maire.	*You **wrote** to the mayor.*
Tu **n'as pas écrit** au maire.	*You **did not write** to the mayor.*
Vous **avez voté** ce matin.	*You **voted** this morning.*
Vous **n'avez pas voté** ce matin.	*You **did not vote** this morning.*
N'avez-vous **pas voté** ce matin?	***Didn't** you **vote** this morning?*

The passé composé with the verb avoir

Most verbs require the auxiliary **avoir** (*to have*) in the **passé composé**:

avoir	to have
j'ai	*I have*
tu as	*you have*
il/elle a	*he/she has*
nous avons	*we have*
vous avez	*you have*
ils/elles ont	*they have*

When **avoir** is used with the **passé composé**, with one exception discussed in the following note, the past participle does not agree in gender or number with the subject of the verb:

J'**ai rapporté** un sac en cuir du Maroc.	*I brought back a leather bag from Morocco.*
Nous **avons décidé** de déménager.	*We have decided to move.*
Tu **as dormi** pendant tout le trajet.	*You slept throughout the trip.*
Avez-vous **réfléchi** à ma proposition?	*Did you think about my offer?*
Anaïs **a vendu** sa voiture hier.	*Anaïs sold her car yesterday.*
Ils **ont entendu** une grosse explosion.	*They heard a big explosion.*

NOTE: When **avoir** is the auxiliary, the past participle agrees with the direct object only when it precedes the verb.

J'ai **lu** une biographie de Marguerite Duras.	*I read a biography of Marguerite Duras.*
Je l'ai **lue**.	*I read it.*
Mathias a **vendu** les vieilles chaises en bois.	*Mathias sold the old wooden chairs.*
Mathias les a **vendues**.	*Mathias sold them.*

*Put the verbs in parentheses into the **passé composé**.*

1. Julien _____ tous les caramels. (manger)

2. Nous _____ le bus sous la pluie. (attendre)

3. Le chien _____ à son maître. (obéir)

4. Les spectateurs _____ les acrobates. (applaudir)

5. Je _____ de steak tartare, mais du poisson! (ne pas commander)

6. _____-vous _____ à l'invitation? (répondre)

7. Les enfants _____ à la pièce de théâtre. (participer)

8. Aurélie _____ le téléphone sonner depuis le jardin. (entendre)

9. Quelle maison _____-tu _____ pour les vacances? (louer)

10. Elsa _____ avant d'agir. (ne pas réfléchir)

The irregular past participles

Many verbs conjugated with **avoir** in the **passé composé** have irregular past participles. This should not come as a surprise, since all these verbs are irregular and need to be memorized. Although not very numerous, irregular verbs are frequently used in French:

apprendre	*to learn*	appris	*learned*
asseoir	*to sit, set*	assis	*sat*
avoir	*to have*	eu	*had*
boire	*to drink*	bu	*drunk*
comprendre	*to understand*	compris	*understood*
conduire	*to drive*	conduit	*driven*
connaître	*to know*	connu	*known*
courir	*to run*	couru	*run*
croire	*to believe*	cru	*believed*
craindre	*to fear*	craint	*feared*
découvrir	*to discover*	découvert	*discovered*
devoir	*must*	dû	*had to*
dire	*to say*	dit	*said*
écrire	*to write*	écrit	*written*
être	*to be*	été	*been*
faire	*to do, to make*	fait	*done, made*
falloir	*to have to*	fallu	*had to*
lire	*to read*	lu	*read*
mettre	*to put*	mis	*put*
offrir	*to offer*	offert	*offered*
ouvrir	*to open*	ouvert	*opened*
peindre	*to paint*	peint	*painted*

plaire	*to please*	plu	*pleased*
pleuvoir	*to rain*	plu	*rained*
pouvoir	*can, to be able to*	pu	*could*
prendre	*to take*	pris	*taken*
recevoir	*to receive*	reçu	*received*
rire	*to laugh*	ri	*laughed*
savoir	*to know*	su	*known*
souffrir	*to suffer*	souffert	*suffered*
suivre	*to follow*	suivi	*followed*
vivre	*to live*	vécu	*lived*
voir	*to see*	vu	*seen*
vouloir	*to want*	voulu	*wanted*

José **a compris** leur explication.
Avez-vous jamais **pris** l'Airbus A380?
Son arrière-grand-mère **a vécu**
  jusqu'à cent ans.
Le film t'**a plu**?
Vous **avez dû passer** beaucoup de temps
  à faire ce film.
Quel cours **as**-tu **suivi** le semestre
  dernier?

José **understood** their explanation.
Have you ever **taken** the Airbus A380?
Her great-grandmother **lived** to be a
  hundred.
Did you **enjoy** the film?
You **must have spent** a lot of time making
  this film.
What course **did** you **take** last semester?

EXERCICE
5·2

*Translate the following sentences into the **passé composé**, using the inversion form when necessary and translating you as **tu**.*

1. Lisa has painted her Maine coon cat.

   _____

2. Did you see my handbag?

   _____

3. We had a drink in the café Les Deux Magots.

   _____

4. Sacha and Juliette spent three years in India.

   _____

5. Why did you open my mail?

   _____

6. I had to go before the end of the show.

   _____

7. Adam has not read *Les Fleurs du Mal* by Baudelaire.

   _____

8. My cousin Anne ran the New York marathon last fall.

   _____

9. Inès has given her sister a silk scarf from Lyon.

_____

10. We sat down in the grass for the picnic.

_____

The **passé composé** with **être**

In the perfect tense, some verbs require the auxiliary **être** instead of **avoir**. This group of verbs includes pronominal verbs, as well as an arbitrary list you need to memorize. The past participles of verbs conjugated with **être** agree in gender and number with the subject.

aller	_to go_
arriver	_to arrive_
descendre	_to go down_
devenir	_to become_
entrer	_to enter_
monter	_to go up_
mourir	_to die_
naître	_to be born_
partir	_to leave_
rentrer	_to return_
rester	_to stay_
revenir	_to return, to come back_
sortir	_to go out_
tomber	_to fall_
venir	_to arrive_

Il **est parti** en France.	_He **left** for France._
Elle **est partie** en Corse.	_She **left** for Corsica._
Ils **sont partis** en Russie.	_They **left** for Russia._
Je **suis née** à Ajaccio.	_I **was born** in Ajaccio._
Napoléon **est mort** à Sainte-Hélène.	_Napoleon **died** in Saint Helena._
Nous **sommes restées** toute la journée sur la plage.	_We **stayed** all day at the beach._

EXERCICE
5·3

Put the verbs in parentheses into the **passé composé**, using the inversion form when necessary.

1. Héloïse _____ chirurgien. (devenir)

2. À cause des bouchons, vous _____ en retard au rendez-vous. (arriver) (_m. p._)

3. Karine, tu _____ en Alsace? (déjà/aller)

4. Nous _____ chercher nos parapluies. (revenir) (_f. p._)

5. Je _____ d'arroser mes fleurs et elles sont fanées. (oublier)

6. Quand Jonathan _____ de cheval? (tomber)

7. Mes filles _____ le premier janvier. (naître)

8. Adélaïde n' _____ pas _____ longtemps à la réunion. (rester)

9. Ils _____? À quelle heure pensez-vous qu'ils reviendront? (sortir)

10. Romain _____ plusieurs fois pendant la conférence. (intervenir)

Pronominal verbs in the perfect tense

Pronominal verbs are always preceded by the pronouns **me**, **te**, **se**, **nous**, **vous**, **se**. There are four types of pronominal verbs: reflexive, reciprocal, passive, and subjective. A reflexive verb directs action back to the subject. Let's look at some examples:

s'habiller	*to get dressed*
je me suis habillé(e)	*I got dressed*
tu t'es habillé(e)	*you got dressed*
il s'est habillé	*he got dressed*
elle s'est habillée	*she got dressed*
nous nous sommes habillé(e)s	*we got dressed*
vous vous êtes habillé(e)(s)	*you got dressed*
ils se sont habillés	*they got dressed*
elles se sont habillées	*they got dressed*

Je **me** lève à huit heures.	*I get up at eight o'clock.*

In the negative, the negation is placed around the auxiliary verb:

Tu **ne t'es pas** baigné dans le torrent.	*You did not swim in the torrent.*
Ils **ne se sont pas** fiés à elle.	*They did not trust her.*

In the interrogative form, the reflexive pronoun is placed before **être**:

Se sont-ils couchés tard?	*Did they go to bed late?*
T'es-tu brûlé avec le barbecue?	*Did you burn yourself with the barbecue?*

The past participle does not agree when the pronominal verb is followed by a direct object or by another verb:

Célie **s'est acheté** une perceuse.	*Célie bought herself a drill.*
Jade **s'est cassé** le coude en faisant du ski.	*Jade broke her elbow while skiing.*

When the reflexive pronoun in a pronominal verb is a direct object, the past participle agrees with it:

Ils **se sont fiancés** en mai.	*They got engaged to each other in May.*
Elles **se sont** encore **disputées**.	*They quarreled again.*

Let's look now at some reciprocal verbs. A reciprocal verb is used when each subject, in a phrase containing two subjects, is simultaneously the agent and object of one action. If a verb is reciprocal, it would otherwise be followed by the preposition **à** and the past participle does not agree:

Vous **vous êtes écrit**.   *You wrote to each other.*
Nous **nous sommes parlé** avant le cours.   *We talked to each other before class.*
Ils **se sont répondu**.   *They answered each other.*
Vous **vous êtes téléphoné** tous les jours.   *You called each other every day.*

Match the fragments in the two columns to create complete sentences.

_____ 1. Alexandra s'est fait   a. après une terrible dispute.

_____ 2. Ils se sont moqués   b. dès le début.

_____ 3. Justine s'est préparé   c. la tête contre la porte.

_____ 4. Florent s'est aperçu   d. à l'archéologie.

_____ 5. Marc et Olga se sont réconciliés   e. quand il a vu le sang.

_____ 6. Luce et Thaïs se sont perdues   f. un thé.

_____ 7. Tu t'es intéressé   g. de ma nouvelle coiffure.

_____ 8. Elles se sont très bien entendues   h. masser par un kinésithérapeute.

_____ 9. Mon oncle a hurlé   i. dans le métro de Paris.

_____ 10. Nina s'est cogné   j. que sa voiture était restée ouverte.

A passive pronominal verb replaces the passive mood in a passive sentence:

Le vin rouge **se boit** chambré.   *Red wine **is drunk** at room temperature.*
Ça ne **se fait** pas.   *It **is not done**.*
Les frites **se mangent** avec les doigts.   *French fries **are eaten** with your fingers.*

Subjective pronominal verbs have a life of their own. Remember them as exceptions. In all past tenses, subjective pronominal verbs always require **être** as the auxiliary verb. In this tense, the reflexive pronoun precedes the auxiliary. In most cases, the past participle agrees in gender and number with the subject:

Ils **se sont aperçus** de leurs erreurs.   *They realized their mistakes.*
Nous **nous sommes souvenus** de   *We remembered his/her stories.*
    ses histoires.
Ils **se sont évanouis**.   *They fainted.*
Après une heure au gala, vous **vous**   *After one hour at the gala, you got bored.*
    êtes ennuyés.

Of the verbs that normally use **être** in the **passé composé**, a few can also take the auxiliary **avoir**, behaving like regular **avoir** verbs in the **passé composé** and functioning, for all practical purposes, like transitive verbs. These verbs are **descendre**, **monter**, **passer**, **rentrer**, **retourner**, and **sortir**. Note that the meaning of the verb may change depending on whether **être** or **avoir** is used.

Ils **sont descendus** au sous-sol.   *They **went down** to the basement.*
Ils **ont descendu** la commode.   *They **took** the dresser **down**.*

Elle **est montée** en courant.	*She **went up** running.*
Elle **a monté** les couvertures dans les chambres.	*She **took** the blankets **up** to the rooms.*
Tu **es passée** devant chez moi dimanche dernier.	*You **passed by** my house last Sunday.*
Tu **as passé** la nuit dehors.	*You **spent** the night outside.*
Elles **sont rentrées** après minuit.	*They **came home** after midnight.*
Elles **ont rentré** les voitures dans la cour.	*They **brought** the cars **into** the courtyard.*
Je **suis retournée** à la bibliothèque hier.	*I **went back** to the library yesterday.*
J'**ai retourné** la crêpe.	*I **turned** the crepe **over**.*
Elle **est sortie** par la fenêtre.	*She **went out** the window.*
Elle **a sorti** la poubelle.	*She **put** the garbage can **out**.*

EXERCICE
5·5

Put the verbs in parentheses into the **passé composé**, using the inversion form when necessary.

1. Quand vous et vos amis _____ de voyage? (rentrer)

2. Je _____ mon chien sous la pluie hier soir. (sortir)

3. Tu _____ tes vieux jouets au grenier. (monter)

4. Théo _____ la piste comme une fusée. (descendre)

5. Avec qui Mélissa _____ samedi soir? (sortir)

6. Ils _____ en taxi. (rentrer)

7. Nos parents _____ visiter l'université de Montpellier. (retourner)

8. Je _____ un examen de français ce matin. (passer)

9. Isaac _____ par la gendarmerie pour porter plainte. (passer)

10. Elles _____ à l'Aiguille du Midi en téléphérique. (monter)

The **imparfait**

The **imparfait** (*imperfect*) is one of the most complex tenses in French, as it covers a wide spectrum of past actions, at various levels of specificity. This tense is typically used to describe a state of mind or state of being in the past, as well as a continuous or habitual past action.

To form the imperfect, take the **nous** form of the present tense and remove the -**ons** ending, which gives you the stem of the **imparfait**. Then add the **imparfait** endings: -**ais**, -**ais**, -**ait**, -**ions**, -**iez**, -**aient**, to this stem:

demander	*to ask*
nous demandons	
je demandais	*I asked*
tu demandais	*you asked*
il/elle demandait	*he/she asked*
nous demandions	*we asked*

vous demandiez	*you asked*
ils/elles demandaient	*they asked*

lire	*to read*
nous lisons	
je lisais	*I read*
tu lisais	*you read*
il/elle lisait	*he/she read*
nous lisions	*we read*
vous lisiez	*you read*
ils/elles lisaient	*they read*

NOTE: The **-ais**, **-ait**, and **-aient** endings are all pronounced alike.

Verbs with spelling changes in the present-tense **nous** form, such as **protéger** (*to protect*) and **annoncer** (*to announce*), retain those spelling changes for all the conjugations in the imperfect except for the **nous** and **vous** forms. Since these particular endings have a vowel, the extra **e** and the **ç**, which otherwise are added to ensure correct pronunciation, are not necessary.

j'annonçais	*I announced*
nous annoncions	*we announced*
elle protégeait	*she protected*
vous protégiez	*you protected*
tu commençais	*you started*
nous effacions	*we erased*
il mangeait	*he ate*
vous partagiez	*you shared*

Depending on the context, the **imparfait** can be the equivalent of several different tenses in English:

	He was reading.
Il lisait.	*He used to read.*
	He read.

The verb **être** has an irregular stem in the **imparfait**, but the verb **avoir** is regular:

j'étais	*I was*
tu étais	*you were*
il/elle était	*he/she was*
nous étions	*we were*
vous étiez	*you were*
ils/elles étaient	*they were*

j'avais	*I had*
tu avais	*you had*
il/elle avait	*he/she had*
nous avions	*we had*
vous aviez	*you had*
ils/elles avaient	*they had*

Using the **imparfait** to describe background and thoughts

The **imparfait** can be used to establish the narrative context of a story, including historical background, descriptive elements, or any relevant information. This tense may describe a past event, situation, or state of affairs. In addition, the **imparfait** often describes a person's past frame of mind or state of being.

Il **faisait** froid.	*It was cold.*
Le vent **soufflait**.	*There was a strong wind.*
Les rues **étaient** vides.	*The streets were empty.*
La vue **était** impressionnante.	*The view was impressive.*
Ils **étaient** assoiffés.	*They were thirsty.*

EXERCICE 5·6

*Choose the right form of the verbs in the **imparfait**.*

1. Jean-Claude vendais/vendait/vendai des gravures dans son magasin.

2. Tu étais/été/fut allergique au pollen.

3. Je lisait/lisais/lirait beaucoup de vieux livres.

4. Je prenait/prendrais/prenais toujours une boule de glace à la menthe.

5. Est-ce que vous voyagiiez/voyagez/voyagiez en première classe?

6. Le train était/est/fut arrêté au milieu des champs.

7. Perrine boivait/buvait/boirait du thé le matin.

8. Il neigait/neige/neigeait sur la ville.

9. Simon écrirait/écrivit/écrivait un nouvel essai toutes les semaines.

10. Nous n'aviez/avaient/avions pas envie de sortir ce soir.

Common verbs used in the imparfait

Some verbs are more often used in the **imparfait** than in the **passé composé**, as they express a mental or physical state. When they are used in the **passé composé**, they may take on a different meaning. These verbs are:

avoir (*to have*)	**croire** (*to believe*)
espérer (*to hope*)	**être** (*to be*)
paraître (*to appear*)	**penser** (*to think*)
savoir (*to know*)	**sembler** (*to seem*)

Tu **avais** mal à la tête.	*You had a headache.*
Tu **as eu** le bras plâtré pendant un mois.	*You had a plaster cast on your arm for a month.*
Elles **semblaient** très heureuses de leur victoire.	*They looked very happy with their victory.*
Elles **ont semblé** hésitantes tout à coup.	*They seemed hesitant suddenly.*
Il **était** malade.	*He was sick.*
Il **a mangé** un fruit pourri et soudain il **a été** malade.	*He ate a rotten fruit, and suddenly he got sick.*

Using the **imparfait** for habitual action

The **imparfait** is also used for habitual, repetitive action. It describes past events that were repeated in the past. The English *used to* and *would* are translated by the French **imparfait**. The following expressions are indications that you should use the **imparfait**:

fréquemment	*frequently*
souvent	*often*
toujours	*always*
le mercredi	*on Wednesdays*
le dimanche	*on Sundays*
chaque jour	*every day*
tous les jours	*every day*
chaque semaine	*every week*
chaque mois	*every month*
chaque année	*every year*
d'ordinaire	*ordinarily*
d'habitude	*usually*
habituellement	*usually*
régulièrement	*regularly*
comme à l'accoutumée	*as usual*
autrefois	*formerly*
jadis	*in times past*

Vous **louiez** le même bateau tous les ans.	*You **used to rent** the same boat every year.*
Ernest **hébergeait** souvent Sophie le samedi.	*Ernest often **used to put** Sophie **up** on Saturdays.*
D'habitude, les pompiers **intervenaient** rapidement.	*Usually the fire department **intervened** quickly.*

Using the **imparfait** with **pendant**

The **imparfait** is used with **pendant** (*while*) to describe two simultaneous actions in the past:

Isabelle **surveillait** les enfants pendant que j'**emballais** les cadeaux.	*Isabelle **was keeping** an eye on the children while I **was wrapping** the gifts.*
Tu **faisais** la vaisselle pendant que tes frères **essuyaient** les verres.	*You **were doing** the dishes while your brothers **were drying** the glasses.*

The immediate past with the **imparfait**

You have studied the immediate past, formed with **venir** + **de** + the infinitive, at the beginning of the chapter. To describe an action that *immediately preceded another action* at a given time, use **venir** in the **imparfait** + **de** + the infinitive.

Nous **venions d'acheter** les billets quand il a appelé.	*We **had just bought** the tickets when he called.*
Ils **venaient de commander** une pizza quand Sylvia s'est évanouie.	*They **had just ordered** a pizza when Sylvia fainted.*

*Translate the following sentences by using the **imparfait** or the **passé composé** and translating you as **vous**.*

1. We had just left when it began to rain.

   _____

2. The basketball game had just started when an incident took place.

   _____

3. Samuel was walking while his cousins were running.

   _____

4. I was whisking the eggs while you were measuring the flour.

   _____

5. You always reserved a room in the same hotel in Saint-Malo.

   _____

6. In the past, people used a lot of salt to preserve food.

   _____

7. Caroline saw that Diego could dance the tango.

   _____

8. Immediately after the explosion, everybody thought of a bomb.

   _____

9. Xavier and Erwan called their mother every day.

   _____

10. You had just been hired by this firm when the scandal broke.

   _____

Imparfait versus passé composé

The **imparfait** is also used to describe a continuous past action that has been interrupted by another past action. The interruption is expressed by the **passé composé**. For example:

Je **lisais** quand quelqu'un **a sonné** à la porte.	*I **was reading** when someone **rang** my doorbell.*
Agnès **parlait** avec son neveu quand Hugo les **a interrompus**.	*Agnès **was talking** with her nephew when Hugo **interrupted** them.*

When an action had been going on for a period of time before being interrupted, the **imparfait** is used with **depuis**:

> Il **pleuvait depuis des heures** quand le soleil s'**est** finalement **montré**.
> La popularité du président **était en chute libre depuis six mois** quand les élections **ont eu lieu**.

> *It **had been raining for hours** when the sun finally came out.*
> *The popularity of the president **had been plummeting for six months** when the elections took place.*

How to choose

As we saw earlier, the **passé composé** describes a single action completed in the past. We have also learned that the **imparfait** is used to indicate a repeated past action or to describe a person's past frame of mind, situation, or general state of being. When telling a story that recounts past events, whether in conversation or in written form, you will most likely use both of these past tenses, often in the same sentence. Combining them can sometimes be tricky. Let's take a look at several ways in which the two tenses can be used in various contexts:

> J'**ai peint** les chaises ce week-end.
> Je **peignais** le plafond quand Natacha **est arrivée**.
> Cédric **est parti** précipitamment.
> Céline **partait** tous les ans en Sicile.

> *I **painted** the chairs last weekend.*
> *I **was painting** the ceiling when Natacha arrived.*
> *Cédric **left** in a hurry.*
> *Céline **used to go** to Sicily every year.*

EXERCICE
5·8

Imparfait or **passé composé**? *Put the verbs into the right tense.*

1. Ariane _____ (mettre) un imperméable pour aller à son rendez-vous.

2. Régulièrement, Grégoire _____ (brûler) une casserole.

3. Je _____ (recevoir) une invitation pour leur mariage.

4. Tous les étés, des libellules _____ (voler) dans le jardin.

5. Tu _____ (prendre) un bain quand tu _____ (entendre) un bruit bizarre.

6. Morgane _____ (porter) plainte, car sa voiture _____ (disparaître).

7. Enzo et Amina _____ (voyager) souvent quand ils _____ (être) étudiants.

8. Les étudiants_____ (lire) en silence, quand tout à coup un téléphone portable _____ (sonner).

9. Nous _____ (vendre) notre voiture jeudi dernier.

10. Thomas _____ (être) dehors quand l'orage _____ (éclater).

The **plus-que-parfait**

The **plus-que-parfait** (*pluperfect*) is used to report events that had been completed before another past event took place. This tense, often skipped in modern English, should not be ignored in conversational French, because even the simplest combination of occurrences may require the speaker to clarify the sequence of events. For example:

> Quand tu **es arrivé**, j'**avais** déjà **trouvé** deux places pour nous.
>
> *When you **arrived**, I **had** already **found** two seats for us.*

This tense is formed with the **imparfait** of **être** or **avoir** and the past participle of the main verb.

aller	*to go*
j'étais allé(e)	*I had gone (lit. I was gone)*
tu étais allé(e)	*you had gone*
il était allé	*he had gone*
elle était allée	*she had gone*
nous étions allé(e)s	*we had gone*
vous étiez allé(e)(s)	*you had gone*
ils étaient allés	*they had gone*
elles étaient allées	*they had gone*

réfléchir	*to think*
j'avais réfléchi	*I had thought*
tu avais réfléchi	*you had thought*
il/elle avait réfléchi	*he/she had thought*
nous avions réfléchi	*we had thought*
vous aviez réfléchi	*you had thought*
ils/elles avaient réfléchi	*they had thought*

descendre	*to go down*
j'étais descendu(e)	*I had gone down*
tu étais descendu(e)	*you had gone down*
il était descendu	*he had gone down*
elle était descendue	*she had gone down*
nous étions descendu(e)s	*we had gone down*
vous étiez descendu(e)(s)	*you had gone down*
ils étaient descendus	*they had gone down*
elles étaient descendues	*they had gone down*

The **plus-que-parfait** indicates a past action that occurred before the beginning of another past action. Stated or implied in a complex sentence, this idea of anteriority, which the pluperfect expresses, generally appears in the main clause. This tense is used in conjunction with other past tenses, such as the **passé composé**, the **passé simple**, and the **imparfait**.

> Les professeurs **avaient obtenu** l'accord de la directrice pour le projet quand elle démissionna.
>
> *The teachers **had gotten** the headmistress's agreement for the project, when she resigned.*

> J'**avais** enfin **déménagé**.
>
> *I **had moved** at last.*

> Jean ne savait pas que Marie **avait acheté** une maison de campagne.
>
> *Jean did not know that Marie **had bought** a country home.*

In the **plus-que-parfait**, all pronominal verbs are conjugated with **être** and almost all agree in gender and number with the subject.

Nous **nous étions écrit** des dizaines d'emails pendant l'été.	We **had written** dozens of e-mails **to each other** during the summer.
Jean ne savait pas que Marie **s'était remariée**.	Jean did not know Marie **had remarried**.
Le président **avait approuvé** ce projet.	The president **had approved** this project.
Le serveur **avait fait** une erreur.	The waiter **had made** a mistake.
Il soupçonnait que son voisin **avait commis** un crime.	He suspected his neighbor **had committed** a crime.

EXERCICE
5·9

*Put the verbs in parentheses into the **plus-que-parfait** or the **passé composé**.*

1. Louise _____ (tout préparer) quand nous _____ (arriver) à la fête.

2. Je _____ (réparer) la machine que tu _____ (casser).

3. Nous _____ (manger) ce que Grégoire _____ (cuisiner).

4. Mon chat _____ (boire) le bol de lait que je _____ (remplir).

5. Quand ils _____ (découvrir) la fraude, le voleur _____ (partir) depuis longtemps.

6. Guillaume _____ (oublier) le livre qu'Irène lui _____ (réclamer) hier.

7. Comme Boris _____ (manipuler) Jean plusieurs fois, il _____ (décider) de se venger.

8. Puisque le secret _____ (être dévoilé) la veille, ils _____ (commencer) à chercher le coupable.

9. Comme sa traversée de la Manche à la voile _____ (se passer) bien, Éva _____ (décider) de traverser l'Océan Atlantique.

10. Vous _____ (accepter) de témoigner au tribunal quand l'avocat _____ (changer) d'avis.

The simple past tense

The **passé simple** (*simple past*) is the historic equivalent of the **passé composé**, referring to a specific, completed action in the past. It is a very elegant tense found in written narration—classic and contemporary and actually favored by emerging celebrity writers and in formal speeches. You will find it in novels, short stories, fairy tales, biographies, and so on. It is a tense you must absolutely be acquainted with to avoid confusion and misinterpretation of a text.

The **passé simple** of regular -er verbs, such as **rester** (*to stay*), is formed by adding the endings -**ai**, -**as**, -**a**, -**âmes**, -**âtes**, and -**èrent** to the infinitive stem. The stem of **rester** is **rest**-:

rester	to stay
je restai	I stayed
tu restas	you stayed
il/elle resta	he/she stayed
nous restâmes	we stayed
vous restâtes	you stayed
ils/elles restèrent	they stayed

Since the **passé simple** is mostly used in narration, you will most often encounter it in the third-person singular and plural. The usual spelling changes apply to verbs ending in **-cer** and **-ger**, adding a cedilla or an extra **–e**:

Elle **mangea** tout le fromage.	She **ate** all the cheese.
Elle **rangea** ses affaires dans le placard.	She **put away** her things in the closet.
Il **déplaça** des meubles.	He **moved** some furniture **around**.
Il **avança** prudemment.	He **moved** cautiously.

The **passé simple** of regular **-ir** and **-re** verbs, such as **agir** (*to act*) and **vendre** (*to sell*), is formed by adding the endings -is, -is, -it, -îmes, -îtes, and -irent to the infinitive stem:

agir	to act
j'agis	I acted
tu agis	you acted
il/elle agit	he/she acted
nous agîmes	we acted
vous agîtes	you acted
ils/elles agirent	they acted

vendre	to sell
je vendis	I sold
tu vendis	you sold
il/elle vendit	he/she sold
nous vendîmes	we sold
vous vendîtes	you sold
ils/elles vendirent	they sold

Être and **avoir** have irregular conjugations in the **passé simple**:

avoir	to have
j'eus	I had
tu eus	you had
il/elle eut	he/she had
nous eûmes	we had
vous eûtes	you had
ils/elles eurent	they had

être	to be
je fus	I was
tu fus	you were
il/elle fut	he/she was
nous fûmes	we were
vous fûtes	you were
ils/elles furent	they were

Other verbs also have an irregular **passé simple**. Sometimes the stem of the **passé simple** is based on the past participle, but this is not a fixed rule. Here are some of the verbs you should start memorizing in the **passé simple**:

boire *to drink*	il but	*he drank*	ils burent	*they drank*
conduire *to drive*	il conduisit	*he drove*	ils conduisirent	*they drove*
connaître *to know*	il connut	*he knew*	ils connurent	*they knew*
convaincre *to convince*	il convainquit	*he convinced*	ils convainquirent	*they convinced*
courir *to run*	il courut	*he ran*	ils coururent	*they ran*
craindre *to fear*	il craignit	*he feared*	ils craignirent	*they feared*
croire *to believe*	il crut	*he believed*	ils crurent	*they believed*
devoir *to have to*	il dut	*he had to*	ils durent	*they had to*
écrire *to write*	il écrivit	*he wrote*	ils écrivirent	*they wrote*
éteindre *to turn off (a light)*	il éteignit	*he turned off*	ils éteignirent	*they turned off*
faire *to do*	il fit	*he did*	ils firent	*they did*
falloir *to have to*	il fallut	*one had to*		
lire *to read*	il lut	*he read*	ils lurent	*they read*
mettre *to put*	il mit	*he put*	ils mirent	*they put*
mourir *to die*	il mourut	*he died*	ils moururent	*they died*
naître *to be born*	il naquit	*he was born*	ils naquirent	*they were born*
obtenir *to obtain*	il obtint	*he obtained*	ils obtinrent	*they obtained*
peindre *to paint*	il peignit	*he painted*	ils peignirent	*they painted*
plaire *to please*	il plut	*he pleased*	ils plurent	*they pleased*
pleuvoir *to rain*	il plut	*it rained*		
pouvoir *to be able to*	il put	*he could*	ils purent	*they could*
prendre *to take*	il prit	*he took*	ils prirent	*they took*
recevoir *to receive*	il reçut	*he received*	ils reçurent	*they received*
savoir *to know*	il sut	*he knew*	ils surent	*they knew*
tenir *to hold*	il tint	*he held*	ils tinrent	*they held*
valoir *to be worth*	il valut	*it was worth*	ils valurent	*they were worth*
venir *to come*	il vint	*he came*	ils vinrent	*they came*
vivre *to live*	il vécut	*he lived*	ils vécurent	*they lived*
vouloir *to want*	il voulut	*he wanted*	ils voulurent	*they wanted*

EXERCICE
5·10

Put the verbs in parentheses into the **passé simple**.

1. Blanche _____ (être) ravie du bouquet de roses.

2. Il _____ (pleuvoir) pendant toute la semaine.

3. Ils _____ (vivre) à Chamonix pendant dix ans.

4. Je _____ (croire) connaître Ethan.

5. Delphine _____ (devenir) vétérinaire.

6. Elles _____ (manger) avec leurs amis.

7. Je _____ (guérir) rapidement.

8. Tu _____ (naître) au Brésil.

9. Gabriel _____ (admirer) le travail du sculpteur.

10. Joseph _____ (croire) voir un requin.

The future perfect tense

The **futur antérieur** (*future perfect*) describes a completed action occurring before another future action. It is formed with the future tense of **être** or **avoir** and the past participle of the main verb. Agreement rules are the same as for the **passé composé**. Although the corresponding construction is rarely used in English, the future perfect is fairly common in French.

tomber	to fall
je serai tombé(e)	*I'll have fallen*
tu seras tombé(e)	*you'll have fallen*
il/elle sera tombé(e)	*he/she will have fallen*
nous serons tombé(e)s	*we'll have fallen*
vous serez tombé(e)(s)	*you'll have fallen*
ils/elles seront tombé(e)s	*they'll have fallen*

entendre	to hear
j'aurai entendu	*I'll have heard*
tu auras entendu	*you'll have heard*
il/elle aura entendu	*he/she will have heard*
nous aurons entendu	*we'll have heard*
vous aurez entendu	*you'll have heard*
ils/elles auront entendu	*they'll have heard*

J'aurai regardé toutes les répétitions.	*I'**ll have watched** all the rehearsals.*
Ils **seront venus** pour rien.	*They'**ll have come** for nothing.*
Il **n'aura pas réalisé** son rêve.	*He **will not have made** his dream come true.*
Tu **n'auras pas gagné** ton pari.	*You **won't have won** your bet.*

Sometimes there is a choice between the **futur simple** and the **futur antérieur**. For example, if you want to imply that two actions are simultaneous, then both clauses of the sentence will use the **futur simple**. However, the **futur antérieur** is required if you are indicating that one action is occurring before the other. Be careful, the rule in English is different. The **futur** or **futur antérieur** is not used in this case.

Je t'**appellerai** quand mon rendez-vous **sera terminé**.	*I **will call** you when my appointment **is finished**.*
Alexis **voyagera** en Europe dès qu'il **sera** majeur.	*Alexis **will travel** all over Europe as soon as he **is** over 18.*

Match the fragments in the two columns to create complete sentences.

_____ 1. Je viendrai te voir	a. les manifestants partiront.
_____ 2. Aurore étudiera l'architecture	b. je la corrigerai.
_____ 3. Quand j'aurai choisi un cadeau	c. quand tu ne seras plus malade.
_____ 4. Dès qu'il aura trouvé une preuve	d. quand le prix de l'immobilier aura baissé.
_____ 5. Nous irons à Venise	e. aussitôt que nous aurons fini de manger.
_____ 6. La diva chantera	f. Julien contactera la police.
_____ 7. Une fois que le ministre les aura écoutés	g. dès que nous aurons mis de côté assez d'argent.
_____ 8. Je ferai la vaisselle	h. je l'offrirai à mon frère pour son anniversaire.
_____ 9. Lorsque tu auras écrit ta lettre	i. dès qu'elle aura son bac.
_____ 10. Ils achèteront un appartement	j. quand elle aura chauffé sa voix.

Replace the infinitive in parentheses with the correct tense. (See Translations *for the English.)*

La Peau de chagrin, Balzac, 1831

Seule avec elle, je ne _____ (savoir) rien lui dire, oui si je _____ (parler), je _____ (médire) de l'amour; j' _____ (être) tristement gai comme un courtisan qui veut cacher un cruel dépit. Enfin, j' _____ (essayer) de me rendre indispensable à sa vie, à son bonheur, à sa vanité: tous les jours près d'elle, j' _____ (être) un esclave, un jouet sans cesse à ses ordres. Après avoir ainsi _____ (dissiper) ma journée, je _____ (revenir) chez moi pour travailler pendant la nuit, ne _____ (dormir) guère que deux ou trois heures de la matinée.

Mais n' _____ (avoir) pas, comme Rastignac, l'habitude du système anglais, je me _____ (voir) bientôt sans un sou. Dès lors, mon cher ami, fat sans bonnes fortunes, élégant sans argent, amoureux anonyme, je _____ (retomber) dans cette vie précaire, dans ce froid et profond malheur soigneusement caché sous les trompeuses apparences du luxe. Je _____ (ressentir) alors mes souffrances premières, mais moins aiguës; je m' _____ (être) familiarisé sans doute avec leurs terribles crises. Souvent les gâteaux et le thé, si parcimonieusement offerts dans les salons, _____ (être) ma seule nourriture.

Quelquefois, les somptueux dîners de la comtesse me _____ (substanter) pendant deux jours. J' _____ (employer) tout mon temps, mes efforts et ma science d'observation à pénétrer plus avant dans l'impénétrable caractère de Fœdora. Jusqu'alors, l'espérance ou le désespoir _____ (avoir) influencé mon opinion, je _____ (voir) en elle tour à tour la femme la plus aimante ou la plus insensible de son sexe; mais ces alternatives de joie et de tristesse _____ (devenir) intolérables: je _____ (vouloir) chercher un dénouement à cette lutte affreuse, en _____ (tuer) mon amour.

Future tense, conditional mood, and subjunctive mood

Could, should, would
Whatever, whoever, wherever, whenever

The immediate future tense

To talk about what you are going to do, you can use the **futur immédiat**, also called **futur proche**, with the verb **aller** in the present indicative followed by a verb in the infinitive. It can replace the present tense in informal speech. For example:

Juliette **va lire** la lettre de son amie Catherine après le petit déjeuner.

*Juliette **is going to read** her friend Catherine's letter after breakfast.*

Je **vais visiter** la tour Eiffel dimanche prochain.

*I **am going to visit** the Eiffel Tower next Sunday.*

Est-ce que tu **vas prendre** rendez-vous chez le dentiste?

*Are you **going to make** an appointment with a dentist?*

Vous **allez** nous **rejoindre** à midi?

*You **are going to meet** us at noon?*

EXERCICE
6·1

*Translate the following sentences by using the **futur immédiat** and translating you as **vous**.*

1. I'm going to move to Lyon soon.

_____

2. Are you going to drink a coffee?

_____

3. Alexis is going to study Mandarin next year.

_____

4. Lola and Charlotte are going to join us later.

_____

5. We are going to call them right now!

_____

6. The president is going to choose his prime minister.

_____

7. The Coliseum is going to be cleaned up.

_____

8. You are going to buy a new house in the country.

_____

9. Malo and Alice are going to sign the contract.

_____

10. Zélie is going to love this book by Olivier Adam!

_____

The future tense

The future tense in French is used to describe events that will take place in the future.

Le président **arrivera** à Pékin lundi matin.	*The president **will arrive** in Beijing on Monday morning.*
Il **fera** une escale à Dubaï.	*He**'ll make** a stop in Dubai.*

However, the future is also used in other contexts. The future tense can soften an imperative phrase. For example:

Tu me **conduiras** à l'aéroport demain.	*Please **drive** me to the airport tomorrow.*
Vous **nettoierez** tout avant de partir.	*You**'ll clean** everything before leaving.*

The future can also provide a polite form for an immediate demand:

Cette bouteille de sauvignon blanc, ça **fera** vingt dollars.	*It**'s going to be** twenty dollars for this bottle of white sauvignon blanc.*

We may also use the future tense to make an informed guess:

Qui a fumé toutes mes cigarettes? Ce **sera** Jean-Louis.	*Who smoked all my cigarettes? It **must have been** Jean-Louis.*
Je ne vois pas Marie. Elle **aura pris** le train de dix heures.	*I don't see Marie. She **must have taken** the ten o'clock train.*

To form the simple future, use the infinitive + the endings **-ai**, **-as**, **-a**, **-ons**, **-ez**, **-ont**. With the **-re** verbs, you have to remove the **e** from the infinitive. Irregular verbs pose an additional challenge, for their future stem is quite different and cannot be simply guessed. The irregular group, which includes **être**, **avoir**, **savoir**, **voir**, **aller**, **venir**, and **pouvoir**, must be memorized, because these important verbs are frequently used in the future tense.

1st group: parler	to talk
je parlerai	*I'll talk*
tu parleras	*you'll talk*
il/elle parlera	*he/she'll talk*

nous parlerons	we'll talk
vous parlerez	you'll talk
ils/elles parleront	they'll talk

2nd group: finir — to finish

je finirai	I'll finish
tu finiras	you'll finish
il/elle finira	he/she'll finish
nous finirons	we'll finish
vous finirez	you'll finish
ils/elles finiront	they'll finish

3rd group: écrire — to write

j'écrirai	I'll write
tu écriras	you'll write
il/elle écrira	he/she'll write
nous écrirons	we'll write
vous écrirez	you'll write
ils/elles écriront	they'll write

These simple future endings work with all verbs, but some irregular verbs have irregular stems, which means you always have to pay attention to the particular stem. While there are some similarities between different irregular stems, reasoning by analogy will not enable you to guess an unknown stem on the basis of the one you know.

acheter	j'achèterai	I'll buy
aller	j'irai	I'll go
appeler	j'appellerai	I'll call
cueillir	je cueillerai	I'll pick
courir	je courrai	I'll run
devoir	je devrai	I'll have to
employer	j'emploierai	I'll use, I'll hire
envoyer	j'enverrai	I'll send
essayer	j'essaierai	I'll try
faire	je ferai	I'll do
falloir	il faudra	one will have to
jeter	je jetterai	I'll throw
mourir	je mourrai	I'll die
payer	je paierai/payerai	I'll pay
pleuvoir	il pleuvra	it'll rain
pouvoir	je pourrai	I'll be able to
recevoir	je recevrai	I'll receive
s'asseoir	je m'assoirai	I'll sit
savoir	je saurai	I'll know
tenir	je tiendrai	I'll hold
valoir	il vaudra	it will be worth
venir	je viendrai	I'll come
voir	je verrai	I'll see
vouloir	je voudrai	I'll want

The verbs être (*to be*) and avoir (*to have*)

Naturally, given the importance of auxiliary verbs in this tense, their future stems need to be thoroughly mastered:

être	to be
je serai	*I'll be*
tu seras	*you'll be*
il/elle sera	*he/she'll be*
nous serons	*we'll be*
vous serez	*you'll be*
ils/elles seront	*they'll be*

avoir	to have
j'aurai	*I'll have*
tu auras	*you'll have*
il/elle aura	*he/she'll have*
nous aurons	*we'll have*
vous aurez	*you'll have*
ils/elles auront	*they'll have*

In English, as we know, in a future tense complex sentence, the dependent clause is in the present tense. French seems to be more literal, because both clauses in a future tense complex sentence require the future tense. Here are some examples:

J'achèterai une nouvelle voiture quand mon frère me **prêtera** de l'argent.	*I will buy a new car when my brother **lends** me the money.*
Nous prendrons une decision dès que Lionel **arrivera**.	*We'll make a decision as soon as Lionel **arrives**.*
Étienne finira son tableau aussitôt qu'il **aura** plus de peinture.	*Étienne will finish his painting as soon as he **gets** more paint.*
Nous irons en ville dès que notre voiture **sera réparée**.	*We will go to the city center as soon as our car **is fixed**.*
Le professeur commencera son cours lorsque les étudiants **se tairont**.	*The professor will start to teach when the students **stop talking**.*

Incidentally, a compound future sentence in English, a type of sentence consisting of two independent clauses, keeps the future tense in both clauses:

Je **ferai** une promenade après le déjeuner, puis **j'irai** au cinéma.	*I**'ll go** for a walk after lunch, and then I**'ll go** to the movies.*

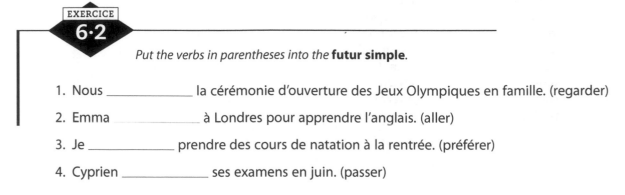

EXERCICE
6·2

*Put the verbs in parentheses into the **futur simple**.*

1. Nous _____ la cérémonie d'ouverture des Jeux Olympiques en famille. (regarder)

2. Emma _____ à Londres pour apprendre l'anglais. (aller)

3. Je _____ prendre des cours de natation à la rentrée. (préférer)

4. Cyprien _____ ses examens en juin. (passer)

5. Zoé et Tristan _____ faire du vélo. (vouloir)

6. Vous _____ par cœur les verbes irréguliers. (apprendre)

7. Camille _____ sûrement plus grande que sa mère. (être)

8. Maxime _____ un nouvel ordinateur pendant les soldes. (acheter)

9. Tu _____ l'été prochain. (revenir)

10. Je _____ de peindre le mur dès qu'il y _____ du soleil. (finir/avoir)

The present conditional

The **conditionnel présent** (*present conditional*) is used to express a wish or a suggestion, but also a statement or a polite request.

Apolline **voudrait habiter** en Italie.	*Apolline **would like to live** in Italy.*
Pourrais-tu **ouvrir** la porte au facteur?	***Could** you **open** the door to the mailman?*

When a condition is implied, the main clause is in the **conditionnel présent** and the **si** clause is in the **imparfait**. For example:

Je **cultiverais** des tomates si j'**avais** un jardin.	*I **would grow** tomatoes if I **had** a garden.*
Le maire **construirait** un stade s'il **pouvait obtenir** plus de fonds.	*The mayor **would build** a stadium if he **could get** more funding.*

The present conditional is formed by adding the endings of the imperfect (**-ais**, **-ais**, **-ait**, **-ions**, **-iez**, **-aient**) to the future stem of the verb. With the **-re** verbs, you have to remove the **e** from the infinitive.

1st group: chanter	to sing
je chanterais	*I would sing*
tu chanterais	*you would sing*
il/elle chanterait	*he/she would sing*
nous chanterions	*we would sing*
vous chanteriez	*you would sing*
ils/elles chanteraient	*they would sing*

2nd group: choisir	to choose
je choisirais	*I would choose*
tu choisirais	*you would choose*
il/elle choisirait	*he/she would choose*
nous choisirions	*we would choose*
vous choisiriez	*you would choose*
ils/elles choisiraient	*they would choose*

3rd group: prendre	to take
je prendrais	*I would take*
tu prendrais	*you would take*
il/elle prendrait	*he/she would take*
nous prendrions	*we would take*
vous prendriez	*you would take*
ils/elles prendraient	*they would take*

Here, too, you need to remember that the verbs **être** and **avoir** are irregular:

être	*to be*
je serais	*I would be*
tu serais	*you would be*
il/elle serait	*he/she would be*
nous serions	*we would be*
vous seriez	*you would be*
ils/elles seraient	*they would be*

avoir	*to have*
j'aurais	*I would have*
tu aurais	*you would have*
il/elle aurait	*he/she would have*
nous aurions	*we would have*
vous auriez	*you would have*
ils/elles auraient	*they would have*

EXERCICE 6·3

*Put verbs in parentheses into the **conditionnel présent**.*

1. Les ours polaires _____ menacés de disparition. (être)

2. Manon _____ rencontrer Ananda Devi. (vouloir)

3. Nous _____ au bord de la mer si nous pouvions. (habiter)

4. _____ on se retrouver devant l'Opéra? (pouvoir)

5. Edgar _____ enlever son nœud papillon, car il a chaud. (aimer)

6. À ta place, je _____ dès maintenant. (partir)

7. Si Boris aimait vraiment Flora, il lui _____ des fleurs. (offrir)

8. _____ vous de corriger ma thèse? (accepter)

9. Le vaccin contre la grippe _____ être obligatoire. (devoir)

10. Il n'y _____ pas autant de poussière si tu faisais le ménage plus souvent. (avoir)

The conditional past

The **conditionnel passé** (*conditional past*) is a compound tense used to describe a hypothetical past event that would have happened, or would have been avoided, if specific conditions had been satisfied. It is formed with the present conditional of **être** or **avoir** and the past participle of the main verb. Keep in mind the rules of agreement that compound-tense phrases may not transgress.

aller	*to go*
je serais allé(e)	*I would have gone*
tu serais allé(e)	*you would have gone*

il/elle serait allé(e)	*he/she would have gone*
nous serions allé(e)s	*we would have gone*
vous seriez allé(e)(s)	*you would have gone*
ils/elles seraient allé(e)s	*they would have gone*

mettre	to put
j'aurais mis	*I would have put*
tu aurais mis	*you would have put*
il aurait mis	*he/she would have put*
nous aurions mis	*we would have put*
vous auriez mis	*you would have put*
ils auraient mis	*they would have put*

EXERCICE
6·4

*Put the verbs in parentheses into the **conditionnel passé**.*

1. Je _____ vérifier moi-même si on pouvait se baigner dans ce lac. (devoir)

2. D'après sa femme, il ne _____ aucune lettre de la banque. (recevoir)

3. Si nous avions su que les chiens s'étaient enfuis, nous _____ immédiatement. (venir)

4. Amélie _____ visiter le Jura. (aimer)

5. Vous _____ ouvrir une librairie. (souhaiter)

6. Tu _____ de rhume si tu n'étais pas resté sous la pluie. (ne pas attraper)

7. Elliot et Sonia _____ se perdre dans cette forêt. (pouvoir)

8. Si Laura le lui avait demandé, Nina _____ avec elle. (rester)

9. Tu croyais qu'ils _____ les travaux avant l'été. (terminer)

10. Théo _____ assister à la compétition de judo. (vouloir)

The **conditionnel présent** or **passé** is also used to express unconfirmed or alleged information. In this case, it is called the **conditionnel journalistique**, used in the newspapers and in news broadcasts. It translates the words *allegedly* and *reportedly*.
First in the **conditionnel présent**:

L'Arabie saoudite **signerait** un contrat avec l'Égypte.	*Saudi Arabia **will** reportedly **sign** a contract with Egypt.*
Le roi du Maroc **se rendrait** en Mauritanie la semaine prochaine.	*The King of Morocco **will** reportedly **go** to Mauritania next week.*

Then in the **conditionnel passé**:

La reine d'Angleterre **aurait dîné** avec James Bond hier soir.	*The Queen of England reportedly **had dinner** with James Bond last night.*
Le suspect **aurait tué** son meilleur ami.	*The suspect reportedly **killed** his best friend.*

Match the fragments in the two columns to form a complete sentence.

_____ 1. Une vache   a. seraient plus écologiques.

_____ 2. Les pompiers   b. diminuerait le stress.

_____ 3. Les trafiquants de drogue   c. aurait confirmé la présence d'eau sur Mars.

_____ 4. Ces professeurs   d. seraient fragilisées par la crise économique en Grèce.

_____ 5. Ce mécène   e. donnerait quinze litres de lait par jour.

_____ 6. Les maisons en bois   f. aurait pêché un piranha dans le canal Saint-Martin.

_____ 7. Les économies européennes   g. auraient critiqué la nouvelle réforme de l'Éducation nationale.

_____ 8. La mission européenne Mars Express   h. auraient été arrêtés ce matin.

        i. financerait l'exposition Dalí.

_____ 9. Sourire plus souvent   j. auraient eu du mal à éteindre l'incendie.

_____ 10. Un Parisien

The subjunctive mood

The **subjonctif** (*subjunctive*) is not a tense but a mood. Used to express a person's opinions or feelings, it often refers to wishful thinking, desired outcomes, and hypothetical actions. The subjunctive has four tenses: **présent**, **passé**, **imparfait**, and **plus-que-parfait**, but only the first two are used in everyday speech.

The present of the subjunctive

To form the **subjonctif présent** (*present of the subjunctive*), add the subjunctive endings, **-e**, **-es**, **-e**, **-ions**, **-iez**, **-ent**, to the stem. The stem for **je**, **tu**, **il/elle**, and **ils/elles** is found by dropping the **-ent** endings from the third-person plural present indicative form.

For example, **envoyer** (*to send*): **ils/elles envoient**. The stem is **envoi-**.

j'envoie	*I send*
tu envoies	*you send*
il/elle envoie	*he/she send*
ils/elles envoient	*they send*

The stem for the **nous** and **vous** subjunctive forms is found by dropping the **-ons** from the first-person plural of the present indicative. As a result, for **nous** and **vous**, the present subjunctive and the **imparfait** are identical.

For **envoyer**, **nous envoyons**, the stem is **envoy-**.

nous envoyions	*we send*
vous envoyiez	*you send*

2nd group: réussir	to succeed
je réussisse	*I succeed*
tu réussisses	*you succeed*
il/elle réussisse	*he/she succeed*
nous réussissions	*we succeed*
vous réussissiez	*you succeed*
ils/elles réussissent	*they succeed*

3rd group: connaître	to know
je connaisse	*I know*
tu connaisses	*you know*
il/elle connaisse	*he/she know*
nous connaissions	*we know*
vous connaissiez	*you know*
ils/elles connaissent	*they know*

Here are some irregular verbs:

être	to be
je sois	*I be*
tu sois	*you be*
il/elle soit	*he/she be*
nous soyons	*we be*
vous soyez	*you be*
ils/elles soient	*they be*

avoir	to have
j'aie	*I have*
tu aies	*you have*
il/elle ait	*he/she have*
nous ayons	*we have*
vous ayez	*you have*
ils/elles aient	*they have*

aller	to go
j'aille	*I go*
tu ailles	*you go*
il/elle aille	*he/she goes*
nous allions	*we go*
vous alliez	*you go*
ils/elles aillent	*they go*

faire	to do
je fasse	*I do*
tu fasses	*you do*
il/elle fasse	*he/she do*
nous fassions	*we do*
vous fassiez	*you do*
ils/elles fassent	*they do*

pouvoir	can
je puisse	*I be able to*
tu puisses	*you be able to*

il/elle puisse	*he/she be able to*
nous puissions	*we be able to*
vous puissiez	*you be able to*
ils/elles puissent	*they be able to*

savoir	**to know**
je sache	*I know*
tu saches	*you know*
il/elle sache	*he/she know*
nous sachions	*we know*
vous sachiez	*you know*
ils/elles sachent	*they know*

vouloir	**to want**
je veuille	*I want*
tu veuilles	*you want*
il/elle veuille	*he/she wants*
nous voulions	*we want*
vous vouliez	*you want*
ils/elles veuillent	*they want*

In a complex sentence, the subjunctive in the dependent clause will follow a verb expressing a wish or a desire in the main clause. It is important to remember that in a subjunctive phrase the two clauses must have different subjects:

Tu veux faire du ski.	*You want to ski.*
Tu veux que tes parents **fassent** du ski.	*You want your parents **to ski**.*
Ils exigent que nous **soyons présents**.	*They demand that we **be there**.*

The subjunctive is used after expressions of emotion:

Je suis ravi que nous **allions** au concert ensemble.	*I am happy we **are going** to the concert together.*
François est déçu que son scénario **soit refusé**.	*François is disappointed that his script **is rejected**.*

The subjunctive is also used after expressions of doubt:

Nous doutons qu'Annabelle **soit** vraiment heureuse.	*We doubt Annabelle **is** really happy.*
Olivier ne pense pas que tu **saches** **parler** japonais.	*Oliver doubts you **can speak** Japanese.*

Starting with a general statement in the main clause, impersonal expressions rely on the verbal moods in the dependent clause to create a balanced phrase. Consider the difference between *It is undeniable that the moon turns around the earth*, and *It is desirable that Paul **take** his father's advice*. That was a subjunctive in the second sentence. *I wish I **were** a queen* is also a subjunctive. Yes, they exist in English! In French, of course, the subjunctive is part of the basic usage, but in both languages, impersonal expressions follow the same logic: indicative mood verbs follow categorical statements, while the subjunctive is added to any statement containing a modicum of doubt, moral obligation, will, judgment, necessity, or emotion.

Some impersonal expressions are followed by the indicative:

il est certain	*it is certain*
il est évident	*it is obvious*
il est probable	*it is probable*
il est sûr	*it is sure*
il est vrai	*it is true*
il me (lui) semble	*it seems to me (to him/her)*

Some impersonal expressions are followed by the subjunctive:

cela me gêne	*it bothers me*
cela me fait plaisir	*I am delighted*
cela ne vaut pas la peine	*it is not worth it*
il arrive	*it happens*
il est bizarre	*it is odd*
il est bon	*it is a good thing*
il est dommage	*it is a shame*
il est étonnant	*it is amazing*
il est étrange	*it is strange*
il est important	*it is important*
il est indispensable	*it is essential*
il est inhabituel	*it is unusual*
il est juste	*it is fair*
il est mauvais	*it is a bad thing*
il est naturel	*it is natural*
il est normal	*it is normal*
il est peu probable	*it is unlikely*
il est possible	*it is possible*
il est préférable	*it is preferable*
il est rare	*it is rare*
il est regrettable	*it is unfortunate*
il est souhaitable	*it is desirable*
il est surprenant	*it is surprising*
il est triste	*it is sad*
il est utile	*it is useful*
il faut	*one must*
il n'y a aucune chance	*there is no chance*
il se peut	*it may be*
il vaut mieux	*it is better*

EXERCICE 6·6

*Put the verbs in parentheses into the **subjonctif présent**.*

1. Mes parents regrettent que nous _____ si loin. (habiter)

2. Je ne crois pas que Margaux _____ travailler dans un cirque. (vouloir)

3. Il est étonnant que le directeur ne _____ rien au sujet de cette dispute. (savoir)

4. Tu as travaillé pendant des jours pour que la fête _____ réussie. (être)

5. Pourvu que Louis _____ mon paquet à temps! (recevoir)

6. C'est la meilleure cuisinière que je _____. (connaître)

7. Victor ira cueillir des cerises à moins qu'il _____. (pleuvoir)

8. Il est possible que nous _____ en retard à la réunion. (arriver)

9. Le règlement de cette école exige que les élèves _____ leurs propres livres. (avoir)

10. Mon cousin est ravi que je _____ acceptée pour ce poste. (être)

The past subjunctive

The **subjonctif passé** (*past subjunctive*) is formed by the **subjonctif présent** of **avoir** or **être** + the past participle of the verb. For example:

s'endormir	*to fall asleep*
je me sois endormi(e)	*I fell asleep*
tu te sois endormi(e)	*you fell asleep*
il/elle se soit endormi(e)	*he/she fell asleep*
nous nous soyons endormi(e)s	*we fell asleep*
vous vous soyez endormi(e)(s)	*you fell asleep*
ils/elles se soient endormi(e)s	*they fell asleep*

dire	*to say*
j'aie dit	*I have said*
tu aies dit	*you have said*
il/elle ait dit	*he/she have said*
nous ayons dit	*we have said*
vous ayez dit	*you have said*
ils/elles aient dit	*they have said*

The imperfect of the subjunctive

Rarely used in everyday speech, the imperfect of the subjunctive is nevertheless very much alive in literature and academic discourse. Journalists will use the imperfect subjunctive, but mostly in the third person. For example:

Le public attendait que Cecilia Bartoli **chantât** une aria de Monteverdi.	*The audience was waiting for Cecilia Bartoli **to sing** an aria by Monteverdi.*

As you know, the verb **chanter** belongs to the first group:

1st group: décider	*to decide*
je décidasse	*I decide/decided*
tu décidasses	*you decide/decided*
il/elle décidât	*he/she decide/decided*
nous décidassions	*we decide/decided*
vous décidassiez	*you decide/decided*
ils/elles décidassent	*they decide/decided*

The following phrase, which includes a 2nd-group verb, may have appeared in a political report:

Le président souhaitait que le premier ministre **partît** immédiatement.	*The president wanted the prime minister **to leave** immediately.*

2nd group: grandir	to grow
je grandisse	I grow/grew
tu grandisses	you grow/grew
il/elle grandît	he/she grow/grew
nous grandissions	we grow/grew
vous grandissiez	you grow/grew
ils/elles grandissent	they grow/grew

Finally, here's an example with a verb from the 3rd group:

Sophie aurait voulu que ses deux enfants **prissent** plus de temps pour songer à leur avenir.	Sophie would have liked her two children **to take** more time to think about their future.

3rd group: apprendre	to learn
j'apprisse	I learn/learned
tu apprisses	you learn/learned
il/elle apprît	he/she learn/learned
nous apprissions	we learn/learned
vous apprissiez	you learn/learned
ils/elles apprissent	they learn/learned

In spoken French, however, the present subjunctive would have been used in the preceding phrase:

Sophie aurait voulu que ses deux enfants **prennent** plus de temps pour faire leurs devoirs de français.	Sophie would have wanted her two children **to take** more time to do their French homework.

EXERCICE

6·7

Re-create the sentences, replacing the present subjunctive with the past subjunctive in the second verb.

1. Je suis content que ma sœur rentre à l'université. (rentrer)

   _____

2. Julie n'est pas convaincue que Guillaume soit un bon conducteur. (être)

   _____

3. Il est surprenant que tu manques le cours de danse. (manquer)

   _____

4. Vous ne croyez pas que ce chien soit obéissant. (être)

   _____

5. Il est regrettable que je ne sache pas changer une roue de voiture. (savoir)

   _____

6. Nous souhaitons que les médicaments fonctionnent. (fonctionner)

   _____

7. Tu doutes que la police retrouve le voleur. (retrouver)

_____

8. Cela me fait plaisir que vous soyez présents à mon mariage. (être)

_____

9. Ma tante est ravie que nous participions au voyage. (participer)

_____

10. Il se peut que les chercheurs fassent une fantastique découverte. (faire)

_____

EXERCICE
6·8

*Translate the following sentences by using the **subjonctif passé** or **imparfait** and translating you as **tu**.*

1. Arthur is sorry that Sarah lost her job.

_____

2. I am delighted that we visited the cathedral of Rouen.

_____

3. The parents wanted their child to grow up in the country.

_____

4. Victoire may have already read the new book by [**de**] David Foenkinos.

_____

5. We are surprised that Max sold all his works of art.

_____

6. You fear that I did not find the keys to [**de**] my car.

_____

7. It is a shame that Anna and Jacob had to leave their apartment.

_____

8. Baptiste did not think that you were responsible for the car accident.

_____

9. It is possible that I misunderstood your explanations.

_____

10. Domitille is furious that her cat broke her favorite vase.

_____

Indicative or subjunctive? Put the verbs in parentheses into the correct mood.

1. Il me semble qu'il _____. (pleuvoir)

2. Crois-tu que le criminel _____ à la police? (se rendre)

3. Le ministre a interdit que ce médicament _____ vendu. (être)

4. Il est évident que Oscar ne _____ pas à l'école. (travaille)

5. Mes parents doutent que je _____ réellement devenir chirurgien. (vouloir)

6. Il est important que vous _____ la situation. (comprendre)

7. Je ne pense pas que ce film _____ intéressent. (être)

8. Il faut que Chloé _____ une université. (choisir)

9. Cela me gêne que tu _____ de nuit. (conduire)

10. Il est étrange que nous ne _____ aucun bruit. (entendre)

Could, should, would

Because *could*, *should*, and *would* have different meanings in English, there is more than one way of translating them into French.

Could

When *could* denotes a specific action at some point in the past, one should, when translating the phrase from English into French, use the **passé composé** of the verb **pouvoir**:

j'ai pu	*I could*
tu as pu	*you could*
il/elle a pu	*he/she could*
nous avons pu	*we could*
vous avez pu	*you could*
ils/elles ont pu	*they could*

Je **n'ai pas pu** vous appeler.	*I **could not call** you.*
Paul **n'a pas pu assister** à la réunion.	*Paul **could not attend** the meeting.*

When *could* describes or implies a habitual action in the past, the **imparfait** of **pouvoir** is used:

je pouvais	*I could*
tu pouvais	*you could*
il/elle pouvait	*he/she could*
nous pouvions	*we could*
vous pouviez	*you could*
ils/elles pouvaient	*they could*

À cette époque-là, les femmes **ne pouvaient pas sortir** dans la rue sans chapeau.	*At that time, women **could not go out** on the street without a hat.*

Quand Léa avait dix ans, elle **pouvait rester** des heures à jouer dans la mer.	*When Léa was ten years old, she **could stay** in the ocean playing for hours.*

When *could* describes a desired future action, an idea, a hypothesis, or a suggestion, the **conditionnel présent** of **pouvoir** is the appropriate tense:

je pourrais	*I could*
tu pourrais	*you could*
il/elle pourrait	*he/she could*
nous pourrions	*we could*
vous pourriez	*you could*
ils/elles pourraient	*they could*

Adrien **pourrait être** plus poli avec les voisins.	*Adrian **could be** more polite to the neighbors.*
Pourrais-tu **venir me chercher** à la gare demain soir?	***Could** you **pick me up** at the station tomorrow night?*

Could is also used in the **conditionnel passé** for a sense of regret, remorse, or reproach:

Tu **aurais pu** me le dire avant!	*You **could have** told me sooner!*
Nous **aurions pu** vous aider, mais personne ne nous a contactés.	*We **could have** helped you but no one contacted us.*

Should

When *should* means *ought to*, either the **conditionnel présent** or the **conditionnel passé** should be used.

je devrais	*I should*
tu devrais	*you should*
il/elle devrait	*he/she should*
nous devrions	*we should*
vous devriez	*you should*
ils/elles devraient	*they should*
j'aurais dû	*I should have*
tu aurais dû	*you should have*
il/elle aurait dû	*he/she should have*
nous aurions dû	*we should have*
vous auriez dû	*you should have*
ils/elles auraient dû	*they should have*

Ils **devraient apprendre** le violon.	*They **should learn** the violin.*
Tu **devrais l'appeler** tout de suite.	*You **should call her** right away.*
Nathan **n'aurait pas dû** espionner son frère.	*Nathan **should not have spied** on his brother.*
Tu **n'aurais pas dû acheter** ce cadre. C'est vraiment laid.	*You **should not have bought** this frame. It's really ugly.*

Would

When *would* refers to a repeated action occurring during a particular period in the past in an English sentence, the **imparfait** should be used in French:

Quand Diane habitait à Paris, elle **traversait** le jardin du Luxembourg tous les jours.	*When Diane lived in Paris, she **would walk** through the Luxemburg Garden every day.*

Lorsqu'elle travaillait chez LVMH,
    Maryse **gagnait** beaucoup d'argent.

*When she worked at LVMH, Maryse **used to**
    make a lot of money.*

When *would* is part of a polite request, the **conditionnel** is used:

Voudrais-tu me **rendre** un service?
Je **voudrais connaître** votre opinion.

*Would you **mind doing** me a favor?*
*I'**d like to know** your opinion.*

When *would* refers to a specific action in the past, the **passé composé** of **vouloir** is used:

J'ai demandé à Gabrielle de me prêter sa
    voiture. Elle **n'a pas voulu**/elle **a refusé**.
Il a demandé a son fils de laver la
    voiture. Il **n'a pas voulu**/Il a refusé.

I asked Gabrielle to lend me her car.
    *She **would not do** it.*
*He asked his son to wash the car. He **would**
    not do it.*

When *would* refers to a desired future action, a hypothesis, or a suggestion, the **conditionnel présent** of the main verb is used:

Corentin et Rosalie **quitteraient** la
    banlieue s'ils avaient assez d'argent.
Jean **irait** à Venise s'il avait le temps.

*They **would leave** the suburb if they had
    enough money for it.*
*Jean **would go** to Venice if he had time.*

EXERCICE 6·10

Connect the fragments in the two columns to create complete sentences.

1. Pourrais-tu

2. Quand nous étions enfants,

3. J'ai mal à la gorge, je n'aurais pas dû

4. Béatrice serait moins fatiguée

5. Ma mère voulait acheter un chat

6. En ce temps-là, on pouvait

7. Ils devraient

8. Si vous lisiez le journal,

9. Quand j'avais un potager,

10. Noé n'a pas pu

a. faire du vélo sans danger.

b. mais mon père n'a pas voulu.

c. arrêter de se disputer.

d. je cultivais mes propres salades.

e. vous seriez mieux informés.

f. si elle faisait moins la fête.

g. prendre une telle décision!

h. m'expliquer la leçon de mathématiques?

i. crier.

j. nous adorions dormir sous la tente.

Whatever, whoever, wherever, whenever

Whatever (**quoi que**, **quel/quelle que**), *whoever* (**qui que**), and *wherever* (**où que**) are used to express concession. They should not be confused with **quelque**, meaning *some* in English, and **quoique**, meaning *although*. All but *wherever* are used with the subjunctive mode. Let's look at *whatever* followed by a verb:

Quoi qu'il fasse, le patron se plaint.
Quoi que vous entendiez à son sujet,
    ne le croyez pas!

***Whatever he does**, the boss complains.*
***Whatever you hear about him**, do not
    believe it!*

Quoi que isn't quoique!

Students sometimes forget that **quoi que** and **quoique** are completely different words! Remember that **quoique**, just like **bien que**, corresponding to the English word *although*, introduces a concessive clause. Note the differences among the following:

Quoi qu'il fasse, son professeur n'est pas content.	*Whatever he does, his professor isn't pleased.*
Quoi que tu dises, il dira le contraire.	*Whatever you say, he'll say the opposite.*

and

Quoiqu'il travaille bien, son professeur n'est pas content.	*Although he is studious, his professor isn't pleased.*
Quoique tu dises la vérité, il ne te croit pas.	*Although you are telling the truth, he does not believe you.*

Indeed, the professor will not be pleased if you forget the difference between **quoi que** and **quoique**!

When *whatever* is followed by a noun, use **quel que** (**quelle que**, **quels que**, **quelles que**) + the subjunctive of **être** + the noun. **Quel que** agrees in gender and number with the noun it refers to.

Quel que soit le prix, nous achèterons cette villa.	*Whatever the price, we will buy this villa.*
Quelle que soit ton opinion, je m'en fiche.	*Whatever your opinion, I don't care.*
Quels que soient les risques, Jérémie atteindra le sommet du Mont Blanc.	*Whatever the risks, Jérémie will reach the top of Mont Blanc.*
Quelles que soient tes habitudes, tu vas devoir t'adapter à cette nouvelle vie.	*Whatever your habits, you will have to adapt to this new life.*
Qui que vous soyez, vous ne me faites pas peur.	*Whoever you are, I am not afraid of you.*
Qui que vous soyez, vous devrez vous soumettre aux directives.	*Whoever you are, you will have to accept the instructions.*
Où que Catherine aille, elle prend des photos originales.	*Wherever Catherine goes, she takes unusual pictures.*
Où qu'Athéna et Ulysse aillent, ils perdent toujours quelque chose.	*Wherever Athena and Ulysses go, they always lose something.*

In order to convey the idea of *whenever* in a French sentence, we can use the following construction: **chaque fois que** + subject + verb in indicative mood.

Chaque fois que je vois David, ça me remonte le moral.	*Whenever I see David, it cheers me up.*
Chaque fois que nous allons à Lille, il pleut.	*Whenever we go to Lille, it's raining.*

EXERCICE
6·11

*Translate the following sentences, using the **tu** or **vous** form as indicated.*

1. Wherever you go, take me with you. (**tu**)

_____

2. Whatever her eccentric ideas may be, she'll succeed.

_____

3. Whoever you are, follow the rule! (**vous**)

_____

4. Whatever the gift, Maylis will be happy.

_____

5. Whatever you do, do it with love. (**tu**)

_____

6. Wherever you decide to live, choose a city in the south of France. (**vous**)

_____

7. Whatever you say, he won't listen to you. (**vous**)

_____

8. Whatever the price of the ring, I'll buy it.

_____

9. Whenever Wolfgang is in Paris, he visits us.

_____

10. Whoever you are, I don't care! (**vous**)

_____

Verb transfers

The concept of *language transfer*, borrowed from the psychology of learning, refers to a technique, conscious or unconscious, that falls back on acquired knowledge to construct a phrase in the target language.

This transfer can be either positive or negative. Here's an example of positive transfer: An English speaker is deciphering a French text. No vocabulary problems, except for the word **idée**, which the reader, after some hesitation, recognizes as *idea*. Since English and French share an enormous number of cognates and even some identical words with similar meanings, positive transfers can greatly facilitate language acquisition within a language family.

Faux amis

Unfortunately, transfers can also go awry, pointing the learner in the wrong direction. How does a negative transfer work? The engine that powers negative transfers, so to speak, is our belief in a mythical parallelism of form and content across language boundaries. If the word **illusion** means pretty much the same thing in English, why shouldn't all shared words be equally accommodating? Well, they are not, because each language relies on a unique alchemy of form and meaning, which explains why the friendly looking word **location** does not mean *location* in English. Linguists have named these problematic pairings *false friends*, or **faux amis**, because they offer nothing but false hope and confusion.

The purpose of this chapter is to debunk the myth that false friends are an unavoidable fact of life. Nothing could be further from the truth. Systematic study, enriched by relevant exercises and pertinent examples, enables you to grasp underlying patterns. For example, take the phrase, "I have made my decision." You probably recognize that this phrase would transfer poorly into French, where a decision is *taken*, not *made*. You may analyze the different mental processes underlying the challenge of decision making in both languages. For example, while the English speaker takes full ownership of the process, in French, it seems that making the right decision is perceived as a question of choosing between several possibilities—in other words, picking or taking the right one.

What makes this chapter unique is its emphasis on verbs, which usually play second fiddle in **faux amis** discussions—usually the emphasis is on nouns. Unlike nouns, verbs express movement, processes, developments, in other words: *change*. Under these circumstances, it is safe to say that verb transfers present an extraordinary challenge for the learner.

Readers may find themselves uncomfortable with the following left-to-right English-to-French format—a departure from our usual format so far in this book. But I've chosen this layout for this chapter because of the immense power—conscious and unconscious—of English syntactic and idiomatic patterns. These patterns are the main cause of negative transfers.

Here are some examples of the negative transfer:

"I returned the book," said Anne to the librarian.	« J'ai retourné le livre », a-t-elle dit au bibliothécaire.

Since Anne returned the book, but didn't turn it over with its cover facing the desk, the correct translation is:

« J'ai rendu le livre », dit Anne au bibliothécaire.

Michael really needs to get into the habit of finishing his homework. Tempting as it may be to start translating this sentence as **Michael doit prendre l'habit de finir ses devoirs**, it would comically undermine the meaning of the original sentence, for in French, **prendre l'habit** means to *take the habit*, that is, *join a religious order*.

Naturally, I am not recommending translation from English into French as a method of learning! However, in certain situations, especially for the native English speaker who doesn't think in French, it is necessary to shed light on the initial stages of forming a French phrase, for they encompass unconscious or barely conscious thought processes that are informed by the speaker's tacit knowledge of rules pertaining to his or her own language. This, of course, does not call into question the fundamental principle that for a bilingual person, learning, so to speak, moves in both directions. Nevertheless, in this particular context, using English as a starting point will, as we shall see, yield many valuable insights.

To *have*

The temptation to overuse this verb, in both languages, should not surprise us: owing to its remarkable versatility and universality, this verb may, covering a wide semantic field, fit into a variety of phrases and expressions. However, count to ten when you feel the urge to "cut and paste" the English semantic field of *have* into a French phrase that *you feel* will work with **avoir**. Remember that highly idiomatic phrases are particularly dangerous. For example: *Thanks for having me* should not be translated as **Merci de m'avoir eu(e)**, for that means *Thanks for playing a trick on me*. The proper sentence is **Merci de m'avoir invité(e)**.

As a rule, French is often more precise than English:

Pierre has many friends among artists.	*Pierre compte beaucoup d'amis parmi les artistes.*

Here are some other examples:

May I have another look?	*Je peux jeter un autre coup d'œil?*
We had a goat cheese sandwich in the park.	*Nous avons mangé un sandwich au fromage de chèvre dans le parc.*
They had breakfast in the garden.	*Ils ont pris le petit déjeuner dans le jardin.*
Ambroise had another serving of egg and bacon quiche.	*Ambroise a repris de la quiche lorraine.*
I had lunch with my best friend yesterday.	*J'ai déjeuné avec mon meilleur ami hier.*
We have dinner at 8 o'clock.	*Nous dînons à 20 heures.*
My grandfather always had a cognac after dinner.	*Mon grand-père buvait toujours un cognac après le dîner.*
Adèle had sex with Jonas last weekend.	*Adèle a couché avec Jonas le week-end dernier.*
Did you have a nice evening with your friends?	*Tu as passé une bonne soirée avec tes amis?*
This summer, they had a lot of visitors in their country house.	*Cet été, ils ont reçu beaucoup de monde dans leur maison de campagne.*

Elizabeth had a good time with her friends in Spain.	*Elizabeth a passé de bons moments avec ses amis en Espagne.*
Have fun!	*Amuse-toi!/Amusez-vous bien!*
Jacques had a hard time last year.	*Jacques a traversé une période difficile l'année dernière.*
I am sure you'll have a very nice vacation in Scotland.	*Je suis sûr que vous passerez de bonnes vacances en Écosse.*
Can I have my books back?	*Tu peux me rendre mes livres?*
Noémie had a pink cap on.	*Noémie portait une casquette rose.*
You've better go now before it starts raining.	*Il vaut mieux que vous partiez avant qu'il pleuve.*
Violaine had her hair cut.	*Violaine s'est fait couper les cheveux.*
The music teacher soon had them all singing in tune.	*Le professeur de musique a réussi très vite à les faire chanter juste.*
"Yvon, you have not done your homework!" "Yes, I have!"	*—Yvon, tu n'as pas fait tes devoirs!—Mais si!*
"You have lied to your sister!" "No, I haven't!"	*—Tu as menti à ta sœur!—Mais non!*
I've had it!	*J'en ai marre!*

To be

Like **avoir** (*to have*), *to be* (**être**) is a verb of great power, since it determines if someone or something is or isn't. One could say that French is less accepting of *to be*, often insisting on a more specific verb in many phrases in which, to an inexperienced learner of French, **être** would seem quite acceptable. For example:

How are you?	*Comment allez-vous?*

Remember, French verbs are more context-sensitive than their English counterpart:

I am well.	*Je vais bien.*
How much is it?	*Combien ça coûte?*
Here's your passport.	*Voici ton passeport.*
Here are your tennis rackets.	*Voici vos raquettes de tennis.*
My sister is afraid of the dark.	*Ma sœur a peur du noir.*
Mathéo is ashamed of his behaviour.	*Mathéo a honte de sa conduite.*
We were very cold last winter.	*Nous avons eu très froid l'hiver dernier.*
I am hot. I think I have a fever.	*J'ai très chaud. Je crois que j'ai de la fièvre.*
My cat Félix must be hungry. He doesn't stop meowing.	*Mon chat Félix doit avoir faim. Il n'arrête pas de miauler.*
You are lucky at card games.	*Tu as de la chance au jeu.*
Julia is forty-three years old.	*Julia a quarante-trois ans.*
How old are you?	*Quel âge as-tu?*
Frédéric, are you sure you're right?	*Frédéric, êtes-vous sûr d'avoir raison?*
They were very thirsty because of the heat.	*Ils avaient très soif à cause de la chaleur.*
Renaud is always wrong.	*Renaud a toujours tort.*
The weather was nice all week long.	*Il a fait beau toute la semaine.*
Ten and two are twelve.	*Dix et deux font douze.*
Émilie is nice, isn't she?	*Émilie est gentille, non/n'est-ce pas?*
"Your brother is going to sue you." "Oh, is he?"	*—Ton frère va te faire un procès.—Ah, vraiment?*
There must be a reason.	*Il doit y avoir une raison.*
It is always windy in Brittany.	*Il y a toujours du vent en Bretagne.*
It's 100 degrees in the shade.	*Il fait 38 degrés à l'ombre.*

*Translate the following sentences using the **est-ce que** form where needed and **tu** or **vous**, as indicated.*

1. We'll have dinner late tonight.

_____

2. Jeanne, can I have my pen back? (**tu**)

_____

3. You'd better buy another cake. There will be a lot of guests at the party. (**vous**)

_____

4. I am so cold! There must be another blanket in the armoire.

_____

5. Here's the book you wanted. (**tu**)

_____

6. Your brother is eight? And he is not afraid to speak in public? (**tu**)

_____

7. The weather is nice in Normandy this week. Have a nice vacation! (**vous**)

_____

8. How much is it? Only twenty euros.

_____

9. Henri is lucky. He got a new job near his apartment.

_____

10. The musician had a blue baseball cap on.

_____

To get

A jack-of-all-trades with no true French equivalent, this verb should be handled very gingerly. Do not translate the phrase *I got it!* as **Je l'ai reçu**, unless you're talking about a package, because the correct translation is **J'ai compris!** Here are some examples:

I got a promotion.	*J'ai eu une promotion.*
You got so many birthday cards!	*Tu as reçu tant de cartes d'anniversaire!*
Timothée got his diploma with distinction.	*Timothée a obtenu son diplôme avec distinction.*
Sabrina got a new job.	*Sabrina a obtenu/décroché un nouvel emploi.*
It's difficult to get a parking space downtown.	*Il est difficile de trouver une place de parking dans le centre-ville.*

Where does your carpenter get his wood?	*Où est-ce que votre menuisier achète son bois?*
Could you get my packages at the post office?	*Pourrais-tu aller chercher mes colis à la poste?*
She got a well-deserved reputation.	*Elle a acquis une réputation bien méritée.*
I am sorry. I did not get your first name.	*Je suis désolé(e). Je n'ai pas entendu/compris votre prénom.*
Got it?	*T'as compris?/T'as pigé?*
The first runner has gotten ahead of his competitors.	*Le premier coureur a pris de l'avance sur ses concurrents.*
My cat and my dog get along very well.	*Mon chat et mon chien s'entendent très bien.*
Claire would like to get away from it all and go to Tierra del Fuego.	*Claire voudrait tout quitter et partir pour la Terre de Feu.*
You should get back home.	*Tu devrais rentrer chez toi.*
Lily got her credit card back.	*Lily a récupéré sa carte de crédit.*
Get down from this tree! You are going to fall.	*Descends de cet arbre! Tu vas tomber.*
Her dismissal got her down.	*Son licenciement l'a déprimée.*
You will get off the train at the end of the line.	*Tu descendras du train au terminus.*
The police got the burglar today. He was having lunch with a friend.	*La police a attrapé le cambrioleur aujourd'hui. Il déjeunait avec un ami.*
Naïm got over a rather serious stomach flu.	*Naïm s'est remis d'une gastro-entérite assez grave.*
I phoned many times but I could not get through to the manager.	*J'ai appelé de nombreuses fois, mais je n'ai pas pu avoir le patron.*
We should get together to discuss the details of the contract.	*Nous devrions nous réunir pour discuter des détails du contrat.*
Get up, it's already ten o'clock!	*Lève-toi, il est déjà dix heures!*
Let's get going!	*Allons-y!*
Yann was not able to get the car going this morning, so he was late.	*Yann n'a pas réussi à faire démarrer sa voiture ce matin, alors il est arrivé en retard.*
Don't hesitate to get help from others!	*N'hésite pas à te faire aider par les autres!*
My kitchen gets a lot of sun.	*Ma cuisine est très ensoleillée.*
Armelle got the flu when she was on vacation.	*Armelle a attrapé la grippe pendant ses vacances.*
I must get my essay to the professor.	*Je dois remettre mon essai au professeur.*
Jean got into the habit of typing his novels on his new iPad.	*Jean a pris l'habitude de taper ses romans sur son nouvel iPad.*

EXERCICE
7·2

*Translate the following sentences using the **est-ce que** form where needed and **tu** or **vous**, as indicated.*

1. Bertrand never got over Paul's death.

_____

2. Tomorrow we must get up at seven to have breakfast with the marketing director.

_____

3. Sonia borrowed a lot of money from you. Did you get it back? (**tu**)

_____

4. There is so much noise here. I did not get your last name.

_____

5. Can you get this novel quickly? I really need it for my French course. (**vous**)

_____

6. Get off the subway at the Louvre station! (**tu**)

_____

7. How did you get the flu in July on the Riviera? (**tu**)

_____

8. We'll meet once a month to talk about the new project.

_____

9. Luc's parents don't want him to get back home after 10 P.M.

_____

10. Where does the baker get his flour? His bread is so good.

_____

To take

While this verb often corresponds to the French **prendre**, you need to watch out for a plethora of connotations, metaphorical and literal, without French parallels. Because *to take* is more versatile than **prendre**, it is imperative to avoid literal translations. For example:

Bus number 12 will take you to the airport.

should not be translated as:

Le bus 12 vous prendra vers l'aéroport.

for that is not a French sentence. The correct sentence is:

Le bus 12 vous conduira à l'aéroport.

Similarly, we may *take a trip*, but being allergic to the idea of *prendre* **un voyage**, a French person will say: **Je vais faire un voyage**. Here are some other examples:

I took his hand.	*J'ai pris sa main.*
Marie-Lys took her daughter by the hand.	*Marie-Lys a pris sa fille par la main.*
Martin took the baby into his arms.	*Martin a pris le bébé dans ses bras.*
Can you take the vase on the shelf and put it in the garden?	*Peux-tu prendre le vase sur l'étagère et le mettre dans le jardin?*
Don't forget to take your passport.	*N'oublie pas d'emporter ton passeport.*
Is this seat taken?	*Cette place est occupée?*
The detective took his name and address.	*Le détective a relevé son nom et son adresse.*
The soldiers took the town in a few hours.	*Les soldats se sont emparés de/ont saisi la ville en quelques heures.*
This novelist takes her ideas from real life.	*Cette romancière tire ses idées de la réalité.*
I take it you have already made your decision.	*Je suppose que tu as déjà pris ta décision.*

I took me three hours to get to Caen.	*Cela m'a pris/J'ai mis/Il m'a fallu trois heures pour arriver à Caen.*
Gabrielle has a foul temper; she takes after her grandmother.	*Gabrielle a un sale caractère; elle tient de sa grand-mère.*
Raoul took apart each of their arguments.	*Raoul a démoli chacun de leurs arguments.*
Selma took back her DVDs.	*Selma a repris ses DVD.*
We slowly took down the pictures.	*Nous avons lentement décroché les tableaux.*
Her plane took off for Rio de Janeiro.	*Son avion s'est envolé pour Rio de Janeiro.*
I took off my clothes before jumping in the swimming pool.	*J'ai enlevé mes vêtements avant de sauter dans la piscine.*
They took us to the opera.	*Ils nous ont emmenés à l'opéra.*
Basil did not take the news very well.	*Basil a été très affecté par les nouvelles.*
I can't take it anymore.	*Je n'en peux plus.*
Take it or leave it!	*C'est à prendre ou à laisser!*

EXERCICE
7·3

Translate the following sentences using inversion as needed and **tu** *or* **vous***, as indicated.*

1. Where are you taking us tonight? (**tu**)

   _____

2. It will take me two hours to finish this translation. (*three possible answers*)

   _____

3. The Grand Palais will take down the Manet exhibition on March 15.

   _____

4. Take the first street on the right! (**vous**)

   _____

5. I am sure Carole will take at least three suitcases.

   _____

6. This seat is not taken. Sit down, please. (**vous**)

   _____

7. Take off your shoes before entering the temple! (**vous**)

   _____

8. Take this bracelet, and put it in your bag! It's a gift. (**tu**)

   _____

9. The children like to watch the planes take off at the Orly airport.

   _____

10. Joséphine is so nice. She takes after her mother.

   _____

To put

Loosely corresponding to the French verb **mettre**, this handy English verb, because it covers enormous semantic ground, often misleads the unsuspecting learner of French, who may be oblivious to this verb's monumental idiomatic productivity. For example:

How shall we put our demands to the boss?

You may have guessed that a French person would never say:

Comment allons-nous mettre nos demandes au chef?

The correct sentence is:

Comment allons-nous présenter nos demandes au chef?

Alexandre put the fan on the table.	*Alexandre a mis le ventilateur sur la table.*
Olivia always puts on lipstick to go out.	*Olivia met toujours du rouge à lèvres pour sortir.*
We put an advertisement in the paper to rent out our apartment.	*Nous avons passé une annonce dans le journal pour louer notre appartement.*
They put us on the train.	*Ils nous ont accompagnés au train.*
I wouldn't put Offenbach on a list of best composers.	*Je ne classerais pas Offenbach parmi les plus grands compositeurs.*
How should I put it?	*Comment dirais-je?*
As Victor Hugo puts it: "To love beauty is to see light."	*Comme le dit Victor Hugo « Aimer la beauté, c'est vouloir la lumière ».*
You put pros and cons. We'll see . . .	*Tu as présenté le pour et le contre. On verra . . .*
Raphaël put a lot of money into this paper factory.	*Raphaël a investi beaucoup d'argent dans cette usine à papier.*
We've put a lot of time into this project.	*Nous avons consacré beaucoup de temps à ce projet.*
Cassandre puts great effort into explaining Latin to her students.	*Cassandre se démène pour faire comprendre le latin à ses élèves.*
I put aside some money to go to Polynesia.	*J'ui mis de l'argent de côté pour partir en Polynésie.*
Put away your toys in the box.	*Range tes jouets dans la boîte.*
After his psychic breakdown, Ivan was put in a mental hospital.	*Après sa crise de démence, on a enfermé Ivan dans un hôpital psychiatrique.*
Put the antique doll back in its place!	*Remets la poupée antique à sa place!*
Benjamin put his hat down and sat in an armchair.	*Benjamin a posé son chapeau et s'est assis dans un fauteuil.*
My aunt Margaud puts down everybody except her darling son.	*Ma tante Margaud critique tout le monde sauf son fils chéri.*
Aurélie put down two thousand euros on a house by the sea.	*Aurélie a versé une caution de deux mille euros pour une maison au bord de la mer.*
The boss put you down as an intern.	*Le patron a mis que tu étais stagiaire.*
They have put in a request for a scholarship.	*Ils ont fait une demande de bourse.*
The filth everywhere put us off.	*La saleté partout nous a dégoûtés.*
I put money on Tornade at the time of the Prix de Diane race in Chantilly.	*J'ai parié sur Tornade au Prix de Diane à Chantilly.*
After everything his brother put him through, he still talks to him.	*Après tout ce que son frère lui a fait subir, il lui parle toujours.*
Mélanie's boss puts her through hell.	*Le patron de Mélanie lui mène la vie dure.*
I'm not going to put up with this behavior! Enough!	*Je ne vais pas tolérer ce comportement! Ça suffit!*

*Translate the following sentences using the **est-ce que** form as needed and **tu** or **vous**, as indicated.*

1. Put your red dress on! We're going out tonight. (**tu**)

_____

2. Will you put an ad in the paper to sell your house? (**vous**)

_____

3. Quentin put his computer down on the desk; then he had lunch.

_____

4. My colleague put aside several personal letters to read after work.

_____

5. Juliette put all the vegetables into the refrigerator in perfect order.

_____

6. Mrs. Deville put all her money into her daughter's new shop.

_____

7. Put everything back in its place before they come back! (**tu**)

_____

8. Jonathan put in a request for financial aid.

_____

9. You need to put down a fifty-euro deposit to rent this bicycle. (**vous**) (**verser**)

_____

10. I put you down as a part-time worker. (**vous**) (**mis que vous**)

_____

To hold

Just like the verbs previously discussed, *to hold* may be related to a particular French verb, which in this case is **tenir**. However, as we already know, the semantic fields of the two verbs may only occasionally overlap, which leaves large areas of uncertainty. It is very easy to step out onto thin ice. For example:

> Jack has never held a job for more than a week.

Which verb should be used in French? **Tenir**?

> *Jack n'a jamais tenu un emploi plus d'une semaine.*

Although a French person would probably understand the preceding phrase, being merely understood is not enough! The correct sentence is:

Jack n'ai jamais gardé/conservé un emploi plus d'une semaine.

Let's look at some other examples:

Can you hold my umbrella?	*Tu peux tenir mon parapluie?*
Noah and Agathe were holding hands.	*Noah et Agathe se tenaient par la main.*
The older brother was holding his youngest brother's hand.	*Le frère aîné tenait son plus jeune frère par la main.*
The wooden stake holds the rosebush in place.	*Le tuteur en bois maintient le rosier en place.*
Audrey's hair was held in place with clips.	*Les cheveux d'Audrey étaient attachés avec des barrettes.*
Everybody holds an opinion about global warming.	*Tout le monde a une opinion sur le réchauffement climatique.*
The nice weather seems to be holding.	*Le beau temps semble se maintenir.*
The press conference will be held in the Japanese garden.	*La conférence de presse aura lieu dans le jardin japonais.*
Antonia and Ingrid are holding a party to celebrate the success of their new company.	*Antonia et Ingrid ont prévu une fête pour célébrer le succès de leur nouvelle entreprise.*
Your car will hold all our suitcases?	*Ta voiture est assez grande pour contenir toutes nos valises?*
Could you hold this money until I return from China?	*Pourrais-tu garder cet argent jusqu'à ce que je revienne de Chine?*
The police held them for the whole night because they were drunk.	*La police les a gardés toute la nuit car ils étaient ivres.*
The police held back the crowd.	*La police a contenu la foule.*
The press held back the number of killings.	*La presse n'a pas divulgué le nombre de meurtres.*
Louis managed with difficulty to hold back his dogs.	*Louis a réussi à retenir ses chiens avec difficulté.*
Hold the line!	*Ne quittez pas!*
Well, well! This is really strange.	*Tiens, tiens! C'est vraiment bizarre.*

EXERCICE 7·5

*Translate the following sentences using the **tu** or **vous** form, as indicated.*

1. We hope the warm weather will hold during the weekend.

   _____

2. A policeman is accused of having held back the name of an accomplice.

   _____

3. The wedding will be held in a nineteenth-century castle.

   _____

4. There are several ways to hold a pencil.

_____

5. Pierre, how can you hold such opinions? You should be more objective! (**vous**)

_____

6. Well, well! Léa and Xavier at the beach!

_____

7. Hold the ladder a minute! (**tu**)

_____

8. My school is holding a party to celebrate its fiftieth anniversary.

_____

9. I am going to try and find Mrs. Bernardin. Hold the line! (**vous**)

_____

10. Olivier will hold these documents until I come back.

_____

To go

While *to go* and **aller** both express the idea of literal (and metaphorical) motion, their numerous semantic and idiomatic differences remain a challenge for every learner. For example, instead of using **aller**, a French person will consider the context and then pick another word. Imagine yourself as a boss telling an employee that you don't need him or her at this time:

> You may go.

Would a French employee understand the literal translation?

> *Vous pouvez vous en aller.*

The correct sentence would be:

> *Vous pouvez disposer.*

Here are some other examples:

How's it going?	*Ça va?/Comment ça va?*
We are going to the Galeries Lafayette.	*Nous allons aux Galeries Lafayette.*
Has Stéphane already gone?	*Stéphane est déjà parti?*
My father always goes too fast on the highway.	*Mon père roule toujours trop vite sur l'autoroute.*
You are pregnant. You can go next.	*Vous êtes enceinte. Vous pouvez passer devant.*
Add nutmeg, stirring as you go.	*Ajoutez de la noix de muscade en remuant au fur et à mesure.*
The children went down the hill full speed.	*Les enfants ont descendu la colline à toute vitesse.*
Justine went up all the stairs to the top of the Eiffel Tower.	*Justine a monté tous les escaliers jusqu'au sommet de la Tour Eiffel.*
Ismaël went on a journey to Turkey.	*Ismaël a fait un voyage en Turquie.*

The ambassador went to a rice field in Vietnam.	*L'ambassadeur s'est rendu dans une rizière au Vietnam.*
My iPhone is gone!	*Mon iPhone a disparu!*
200 workers are supposed to be let go at Moulinex.	*200 ouvriers sont censés être licenciés chez Moulinex.*
After two days in Saint-Tropez, all my money was gone!	*Après deux jours à Saint-Tropez, j'avais dépensé tout mon argent!*
The way things are going, the firm is going to have to file for bankruptcy.	*Si ça continue comme ça, l'entreprise va devoir déposer son bilan.*
The ceremony at the Académie française went very well.	*La cérémonie à l'Académie française s'est très bien passée.*
The Sahara desert goes from Mauritania to Sudan.	*Le désert du Sahara s'étend de la Mauritanie au Soudan.*
$100 does not go very far.	*On ne va pas très loin avec 80 euros.*
What's wrong with Carla? Has she gone mad?	*Qu'est-ce qui ne va pas chez Carla? Elle est folle?/Elle est devenue folle?*
The light went red.	*Le feu est passé au rouge.*
Marc went through a red light.	*Marc a brûlé un feu rouge.*
There goes another crystal glass!	*Encore un verre en cristal de cassé!*
My great-uncle's mind is going.	*Mon grand-oncle n'a plus toute sa tête.*
The opera singer was supposed to sing *La Traviata* but his voice was gone.	*Le chanteur était censé chanter La Traviata mais il n'avait plus de voix.*
The story goes that a princess of Denmark is going to marry a tightrope walker.	*Le bruit court qu'une princesse du Danemark va épouser un funambule.*
Anything goes.	*Tout est permis.*
That goes without saying.	*Cela va sans dire.*
Irina doesn't know how the words of the song go.	*Irina ne connaît pas les paroles de cette chanson.*
Kiyo is not bad, as far as fashion designers go.	*Kiyo n'est pas mauvais comme styliste.*
There are three weeks to go before the swimming competition.	*Il reste trois semaines avant la compétition de natation.*
He had gone only three miles when a tire burst.	*Il n'avait fait que cinq kilomètres quand un pneu a éclaté.*
We were going across the street when suddenly I saw Lyne on the sidewalk.	*Nous traversions la rue quand, soudain, j'ai vu Lyne sur le trottoir.*
Madeleine has gone away on vacation without her cell phone.	*Madeleine est partie en vacances sans son portable.*
We went back to Nepal the third time.	*Nous sommes retournés au Népal pour la troisième fois.*
This story goes back to the 19th century.	*Cette histoire remonte au XIXe siècle.*
You've got to go by the book!	*Vous devez appliquer strictement le règlement!*

EXERCICE
7·6

*Translate the following sentences using the **est-ce que** form where needed and **tu** or **vous**, as indicated.*

1. Her family goes back to Louis XVIII.

_____

2. How did Pierre's birthday party go?

_____

3. I was going across the Boulevard des Capucines when I saw Christian Lacroix!

_____

4. There goes another plate!

_____

5. Louise went through a red light last night.

_____

6. Let's go to Nohant tomorrow. I want to visit George Sand's house.

_____

7. Nora wants to go back to Brazil next year. It will be the fourth time.

_____

8. The prime minister of Great Britain will go to Dakar at the end of the month.

_____

9. The story goes that the prince lied to his family.

_____

10. I can't teach today. My voice has gone.

_____

To keep

Keep in mind that the French equivalents of *to keep* that you might think of, such as **garder**, work only in the right context. Unfortunately, what seems to be the right context in English may often strike a French person as odd, if not incomprehensible. For example, even the simplest English phrase may pose a challenge:

> Pierre kept his promise.

In English, it seems, a promise is like a keepsake, something to be treasured; one is faithful to a promise. However, this idea does not work in French:

> *Pierre a gardé sa promesse.*

The correct sentence is:

> *Pierre a tenu sa promesse.*

Here are a few other examples:

May I keep the cork of this Mouton Cadet 1947?	*Puis-je garder le bouchon de ce Mouton Cadet 1947?*
You must keep the cake in a cold place.	*Il faut conserver le gâteau au frais.*
These peaches do not keep long.	*Ces pêches ne se conservent pas longtemps.*
How long could you keep this Venetian mirror for me?	*Combien de temps pouvez-vous mettre de côté ce miroir vénitien?*
Where do you keep your medicine?	*Où ranges-tu tes médicaments?*

After the accident, Joanne was kept in the hospital for two days.	*Après l'accident, Joanne a dû passer deux jours à l'hôpital.*
This chiropractor has the bad habit of keeping his patients waiting.	*Ce chiropracteur a la sale habitude de faire attendre ses patients.*
I tried to say something, but Leïla kept talking.	*J'ai essayé de dire quelque chose, mais Leïla a continué à parler.*
My secretary keeps forgetting to take down some important messages.	*Mon secrétaire oublie tout le temps de noter des messages importants.*
Her lawyer kept saying I was a bad driver.	*Son avocat ne cessait de dire que j'étais un mauvais conducteur.*
I was holding the ladder to keep Michel from falling.	*Je tenais l'échelle pour empêcher Michel de tomber.*
Keep quiet!	*Tais-toi!*
Keep your stomach in!	*Rentre le ventre!*
Keep out.	*Défense d'entrer.*

EXERCICE 7·7

Translate the following sentences using inversion as needed and **tu** *or* **vous**, *as indicated.*

1. I am sure the clinic will keep Étienne at least a week.

   _____

2. Where do you keep your tea cups? (**tu**) (**ranger**)

   _____

3. We are in a theater. Keep quiet! (**vous**)

   _____

4. This bread won't keep more than three days.

   _____

5. Don't keep me waiting! (**tu**)

   _____

6. Patrick keeps complaining about everything.

   _____

7. Keep the change! (**vous**)

   _____

8. You cannot keep him from seeing his ex-mother-in-law. (**tu**)

   _____

9. Anne promised to keep the secret.

   _____

10. He keeps forgetting to buy olive oil.

   _____

Faire

In the previous sections, we illustrated the numerous discrepancies between English and French verbs by providing examples of incorrect usage caused by the learner's good-natured belief that verbs like to play nice! Well, as you know by now, they play, but as far as their mannerisms are concerned, the word *nice* does not come to mind.

Until now, the English examples on the left side of the page have given you a selection of verbs known for their uncanny ability to attract false friends. So moving from left to right, you were to seek a safe route between Scylla and Charybdis, hoping to land on a friendly French verb.

Let's see what happens when we ask the two mythological monsters to take a break and play a game of Scrabble. On the left, you will still find English sentences with a variety of verbs, which, as you will discover on the right side, all become **faire** in French. The purpose of this particular exercise is not only to demonstrate the productivity of a frequently used French verb, but also to familiarize you with an important part of French idiomatic vocabulary and to enable you to investigate these key verbs on your own.

Can you bake a cake?	*Tu peux faire un gâteau?*
What about going for a walk?	*Si on faisait une promenade?*
I am going to play hooky.	*Moi, je vais faire l'école buissonnière.*
The doctor will probably give you a shot.	*Le médecin vous fera sans doute une piqûre.*
I have several checks to write.	*Je dois faire plusieurs chèques.*
What about a cruise?	*Et si on faisait une croisière?*
Our bedroom is twenty feet wide.	*Notre chambre fait six mètres de large.*
I went around all the libraries, but I could not find the book I needed.	*J'ai fait toutes les bibliothèques mais je n'ai pas pu trouver le livre dont j'avais besoin.*
I am only repeating what Christine said.	*Je ne fais que répéter ce que Christine a dit.*
It has been five years since we last went to Amsterdam.	*Cela fait cinq ans que nous ne sommes pas allés à Amsterdam.*
She is a self-made woman.	*Elle s'est faite toute seule.*
It does not matter.	*Cela ne fait rien.*
Don't worry!	*Ne t'en fais pas!/Ne vous en faites pas!*

EXERCICE
7·8

Translate the following sentences using inversion as needed and **tu** *or* **vous**, *as indicated.*

1. She is writing a check.

   _____

2. The nurse gave me a shot.

   _____

3. It has been three months since I visited my grandfather.

   _____

4. Let's go for a walk!

   _____

5. Can you cook? (**vous**)

   _____

6. I am only telling you what I heard. (**tu**)

_____

7. His living room must be twenty feet wide.

_____

8. I am not worried.

_____

9. It has been a year since she called her sister.

_____

10. Lucie would like to go on a cruise.

_____

EXERCICE
7·9

Select the theme corresponding to each sentence.

activité artistique	communication	cuisine	dessert	études
maison	problème	sortie	sport	voyage

1. Est-ce que Damien fait du théâtre? _____

2. Cela fait six mois que nous ne sommes pas allés au cinéma. _____

3. Ils ont fait plusieurs pâtisseries pour trouver un gâteau original. _____

4. Je ferai une salade pour le déjeuner. _____

5. Vous avez fait toute la Sicile pendant vos vacances. _____

6. La terrasse fait dix mètres carrés. _____

7. Alexandre fait une école d'ingénieur. _____

8. —J'ai oublié ton dictionnaire.—Cela ne fait rien. _____

9. Arrête de crier, je ne fais que te transmettre le message d'Astrid! _____

10. Si on faisait une randonnée dans les calanques de Cassis. _____

A final thought

There is no magic converter that will turn an English verb into its French equivalent. On second thought, there is one: you! To develop your understanding of French verbs, you must study your dictionary with a critical eye. Stopping at the first connotation of a word is for novices! If you have an idea in mind, you must patiently examine every connotation of a target word, even those that seem farfetched, until you get a perfect match. Even if the match is not perfect, this method will show you how to successfully sail the stormy seas of French verbs as you continue your exploration of the forgotten lands of grammar.

Common confusing verbs

As you have noticed so far, the French language is full of surprises. The previous chapter introduced you to **faux amis** (*false friends*), especially as they occur in verbs. In this chapter, the confusion continues—we look at verbs that often confuse English learners of French.

Prêter/emprunter

There is some confusion in English when speakers use the verb *to loan*, without making a clear distinction between the verbs *to lend* and *to borrow*. There is no such confusion in French.

Prêter

Ils **prêtent** à 8%.	*They **give loans** at 10%.*
Pourrais-tu me **prêter** ta voiture samedi?	*Could you **lend** me your car on Sunday?*
Vous devrez **prêter** serment.	*You'll have to **take an oath**.*
Tu **devrais prêter un peu plus attention** à ce qu'ils disent.	*You **should pay more attention to** what they have to say.*
Isabelle Huppert **a prêté** son nom à une organisation de bienfaisance.	*Isabelle Huppert **lent** her name **to** a charity.*

Emprunter

Les Tanguy **ont emprunté** 50 000 euros **à** la banque.	*The Tanguys **borrowed** 50,000 euros **from** the bank.*
Pourquoi **n'empruntes-tu pas** ce nouveau roman **à** la bibliothèque?	*Why **don't you borrow** this new novel **from** the library?*
Ces métaphores **sont empruntées** à la musique baroque.	*These metaphors **are derived from** baroque music.*
Les randonneurs **ont emprunté** un sentier escarpé pour arriver au col du Ventoux.	*The hikers **used** a steep path to get to the Ventoux mountain pass.*
N'empruntez pas ce passage souterrain!	***Do not use** this underpass!*

Poser/demander/interroger/mettre ou remettre en question

These verbs are used in specific ways and are often confused. Most important, remember to **poser une question**.

Poser

Le propriétaire leur **a posé** des questions.   *The owner **asked** them some questions.*
Vous devriez lui **poser la question**.   *You should **ask** him **about it**.*

Demander

Il a **demandé** l'autorisation de créer   *He **asked for** permission to create an*
une association.   *association.*
Elle **a demandé** une réponse d'ici jeudi.   *She **asked for** an answer by Thursday.*

Interroger

La police **a interrogé** le suspect pendant   *The police **questioned** the suspect for*
trois heures.   *three hours.*
Vendredi, vous **serez interrogés par**   *On Friday, you**'ll be given a written test** on*
écrit sur la géographie de la France.   *the geography of France.*

Mettre en question/remettre (se remettre) en question

These two verbs are interchangeable most of the time. It all depends on the context:

Le directeur du marketing **a mis en**   *The marketing director **questioned** this*
question la compétence de ce candidat.   *candidate's competence.*
Un scientifique de renom **met en**   *One well-known scientist **questions***
question cette nouvelle théorie.   *this theory.*
Ce projet artistique **est** sans cesse   *This artistic project **is** continually **being***
remis en question.   ***called into question**.*
Selon Sartre, il est important de **se**   *According to Sartre, it is important **to***
remettre en question de temps en   ***do some soul-searching** now and then.*
temps.

Commander/ordonner

Commander

Mesdames, **avez**-vous déjà **commandé**?   *Ladies, **have** you already **ordered**?*
J'**ai commandé** trois livres et un DVD   *I **ordered** three books and one DVD*
sur Amazon.fr.   *on Amazon.fr.*

Ordonner

Il leur **a ordonné** de se taire.   *He **ordered** them to be quiet.*
Le général **va ordonner** que ce soit   *The general **will order** that it be done*
fait sur-le-champ.   *immediately.*

EXERCICE
8·1

*Translate the following sentences, using **tu** or **vous**, as indicated.*

1. Ask for an appointment for Friday morning. (**tu**)

   _____

2. Paul wants to borrow my car on Sunday afternoon.

   _____

3. Céline ordered a chocolate mousse.

   _____

4. Alexandre continually questions his choice of career.

   _____

5. Can you lend me the notes you took at the conference? (**vous**)

   _____

6. The mayor of Strasbourg has ordered the closing of a discotheque.

   _____

7. This expression is probably derived from the German language.

   _____

8. I would like to ask you a delicate question. (**vous**)

   _____

9. Inès borrowed a dress from her best friend, Noami.

   _____

10. The detective questioned Jean and his brother.

   _____

Apporter/emporter/rapporter/amener/emmener

These verbs indicate someone bringing or taking things somewhere. It is important to use these verbs only with *things*, not human beings. **Apporter** and **amener** start with an **a-**, so the thing or the person comes to the speaker. **Emporter** and **emmener** start with an **e-**, actually an **ex** in Latin, so it goes out, away from the speaker. This is one trick to remember. Some exceptions can be found in literary discourse and abstract statements. However, this is the basic rule you need to refer to in everyday conversation. And be careful, even French people tend to make this mistake. You have to prove them wrong!

Apporter

Apporte-moi une tasse de thé!	*Bring me a cup of tea!*
Le président **a apporté** bien des changements.	*The president **brought** many changes.*

Emporter

Ma tante Jeanne **emporte** au moins trois valises en vacances.	*My aunt Jeanne **takes** at least three suitcases on vacation.*
Dans ce petit restaurant, il y a des plats chauds **à emporter**.	*At this restaurant, there are hot dishes **to take out**.*

Rapporter

Quand voulez-vous que je **rapporte** votre couscoussier?	*When do you want me to **bring back** your couscous maker?*

| Érica **rapportera** une baguette en rentrant. | *Érica **will bring** a baguette when she gets back.* |

Amener/emmener

| **Amène** les enfants chez moi vers dix heures! | ***Bring** the children home around 10 o'clock.* |
| Qu'est-ce qui vous **amène** ici? | *What **brings** you here?* |

Here are some exceptions when **amener** means *to be the cause, to provoke.*

| La sécheresse **a amené** la famine. | *The drought **brought about** famine.* |
| Cela pourrait l'**amener** à démissionner. | *This could **bring** him to resign.* |

Aménager/emménager/déménager

Aménager

Aménager is an important verb to know how to handle. You'll read it in the press every day.

| L'État **va aménager** de nouveaux espaces dans le bois de Vincennes. | *The government **is going to develop** some new areas in the bois de Vincennes.* |
| Le patron **a décidé d'aménager** les horaires de travail. | *The boss **has decided to adjust** the working hours.* |

But you can also use **aménager** at home:

| Florence **va aménager** cette chambre en bureau. | *Florence **is going to convert** this bedroom into a study.* |
| Dans ce catalogue figurent des cuisines **aménagées en design contemporain**. | *This catalog features **fully equipped and modernly designed** kitchens.* |

Emménager

Emménager starts with an **e-**, which indicates that you are going from point A to point B.

| Les Gautier **viennent d'emménager** dans un nouvel appartement. | *The Gautiers **just moved into** a new apartment.* |
| Théo **a fini par emménager** avec sa compagne. | *Théo **finally moved in** with his partner.* |

Déménager

Here comes the problem! **Déménager** simply indicates the idea of moving out of somewhere, not of moving in, like **emménager**. This is a typical mistake. Be aware of it. Remember Théo and Véronique!

| Véronique **doit déménager** avant le 31 mars. | *Véronique **must move out** before March 31st.* |
| L'entreprise **va déménager** ses bureaux sur l'île de la Jatte. | *The company **will move** its offices on the Île de la Jatte.* |

Rencontrer/rejoindre/retrouver/se joindre à

Here are some other tough ones. Here again, the English language is the culprit because the verb *to meet* is so elastic. Look carefully at the examples and familiarize yourself with the nuances.

Rencontrer

As a rule, **rencontrer** is used when you meet someone for the first time or by chance:

Nella et Fabrice **se sont rencontrés** dans un cours de français.	*Nella and Fabrice **met** in a French class.*
J'**ai rencontré** Félicie ce matin au marché aux puces.	*I **ran into** Félicie this morning at the flea market.*

However, in formal situations, **rencontrer** does not necessarily refer to a first encounter. It emphasizes the importance of the meeting, but it does not mean that the persons involved had never met before.

Le Premier ministre français **a rencontré** son homologue britannique lors du Sommet européen.	*The French prime minister **had a meeting with** his British counterpart during the European Summit.*

Rejoindre

Rejoindre means that one person or more will meet another or several persons in a specific place. **Retrouver** is a synonym.

Rejoindre

On **se rejoint** à la gare à midi.	*Let's **meet** at the station at noon.*
Je n'ai pas fini mon article. Je vous **rejoins** tous les deux au Café de la Paix dans une heure.	*I have not finished my article. I'll **meet** you both at the Café de la Paix in an hour.*

Retrouver

Je **te retrouve** devant le cinéma à 19 heures.	*I'll **meet you** outside the movie theater at 7 p.m.*
On **se retrouve** à quinze heures?	***Should** we **meet** at 3 p.m.?*

Se joindre à

When one or more persons join a group already formed, an association, or a club, **se joindre à** is the proper verb.

Voudriez-vous **vous joindre à** nous dimanche pour le pique-nique annuel?	*Would you like **to join** us on Sunday for the annual picnic?*
N'hésitez pas à vous **joindre à** notre discussion! On a besoin de votre avis.	*Do not hesitate **to join** in the discussion. We need your opinion.*

EXERCICE
8·2

*Translate the following sentences, using the **est-ce que** form as needed and the **tu** or **vous** form, as indicated.*

1. We'll have a party at the pool tonight. Would you like to join us? (**tu**)

_____

2. The prime ministers of France and Great Britain will meet in Berlin in May.

_____

3. Lise, you want to take these two huge suitcases for just two days? Are you crazy? (**tu**)

_____

4. Ask Pierre to be at La Perle, rue Vieille du Temple. I'll meet you around 8 p.m. (**vous**)

_____

5. Bring Léonie a nice bouquet of flowers! (**vous**)

_____

6. Rémi is moving out on Saturday. Can you come and help us? (**tu**)

_____

7. I took my niece to l'Opéra Bastille. She loves _Carmen_.

_____

8. You are moving in with Simon! Congratulations! (**tu**)

_____

9. Don't bring your brother-in-law on Sunday! I don't like him at all. (**tu**)

_____

10. Laura's school knows how to adjust the children's schedule to give them more time for arts and sports.

_____

EXERCICE
8·3

Complete each sentence with the appropriate verb, using the **tu** or **vous** form, as indicated.

1. _____ un parapluie! Je pense qu'il va pleuvoir. (**tu**)

2. Je _____ Jérémie pour la première fois, boulevard Montparnasse. Je l'adore!

3. Lila et Loïs _____ en février et se sont mariés en décembre de la même année.

4. _____-moi au bout du monde! (**tu**)

5. Les voleurs se sont introduits dans la maison et ils _____ tous nos bijoux.

6. _____-moi un sari en soie sauvage de Madras!

7. Pars avant moi! Nous _____ tous à la Brasserie Mollard vers 21 heures.

8. Cela me ferait tant plaisir si vous pouviez _____ nous. Toute la famille sera là.

9. J'adore cet appartement. Je refuse de _____ une autre fois. Ça suffit!

10. Le propriétaire du château _____ l'ancienne écurie en quatre chambres d'hôtes. C'est vraiment magnifique!

Arrêter/s'arrêter

A common mistake is the omission of the reflexive pronoun in front of the verb. The verb **arrêter** does exist, but it has a different meaning. Here are some examples.

Arrêter

La police **a arrêté** un dealer de drogue, rue de Verneuil.

Arrêtez la voiture ici!

*The police **arrested** a drug dealer on the rue de Verneuil.*

***Stop** the car here!*

S'arrêter

Je me **suis arrêtée** devant les vitrines de Sonia Rykiel.

Ce train **ne s'arrête pas** à Orléans.

*I **stopped** in front of Sonia Rykiel's windows.*

*This train **does not stop** in Orleans.*

Pousser/faire pousser

More subtleties! Yes, *to grow* is so easy in English. But in French, you must analyze the meaning before making the decision.

Pousser

Katiana **pousse** le landau de son bébé.

Mes tomates **poussent bien** cette année.

*Katiana **pushes** her baby's pram.*

*My tomatoes **are doing nicely** this year.*

Faire pousser

Ils **font pousser** du seigle dans le Massif Central.

Comment **faire pousser** un avocatier à la maison?

*They **grow** rye in the Massif Central.*

*How **to grow** an avocado tree at home?*

Visiter/rendre visite/faire visiter

As a rule, **visiter** is used when refering to places.

Visiter

Roland et moi **avons visité** l'abbaye de Cluny près de Macon.

Nous **avons visité** trois maisons à vendre.

*Roland and I **visited** the Cluny Abbey near Macon.*

*We **viewed** three houses for sale.*

Rendre visite

When you visit someone socially, use **rendre visite à**:

Nous **allons rendre visite** à mes beaux-parents ce week-end.

Éolia **voudrait rendre visite** à ses amis en Italie.

*We'll **visit** my in-laws this weekend.*

*Éolia **would like to visit** her friends in Italy.*

However, if your teeth hurt, you neither **visiter** nor **rendre visite** to the dentist. You simply go to the dentist's:

Tu **devrais aller chez** un dentiste.

*You **should visit (go to, see)** a dentist.*

Visiter can be used when referring to people in a hospital or jail setting. This usage is **discutable**. Although it is correct, today people may just say **aller voir**.

Le Dr Clément **visitera** le patient à l'hôpital demain matin.	*Dr. Clément **will visit** the patient at the hospital tomorrow morning.*
L'avocat **visitera** sa cliente à la prison de la Roquette.	*The lawyer **will visit** his client in the la Roquette prison.*

Faire visiter

Un chercheur du CNRS **m'a fait visiter** son laboratoire.	*A CNRS researcher **showed me around** his laboratory.*
Tu **me fais visiter** ton appartement?	***Can** you **show me around** your apartment?*

EXERCICE

8·4

Translate the following sentences, using the **est-ce que** form as needed and the **tu** or **vous** form, as indicated.

1. Mélanie will visit her friend Léa in Rouen this summer.

_____

2. Push this chair against the wall! (**tu**)

_____

3. Stop asking questions! (**tu**)

_____

4. Inspector Clouseau is so happy today. He arrested Sir Charles Lytton.

_____

5. You must visit the Futuroscope in Poitiers. (**vous**)

_____

6. My uncle grows corn in his garden.

_____

7. Léa's parents showed me around their house.

_____

8. They stopped in a beautiful village in Corrèze.

_____

9. Our cauliflowers refused to grow this year.

_____

10. You need to ask for authorization to visit someone in this prison. (**tu**)

_____

Vouloir/en vouloir à

Vouloir

The general meaning of **vouloir** is *to want, to wish*. It is followed by either a direct object or a verb in the infinitive. When the partitive article and an object are replaced, **en** is used.

Nous **voulons** une réforme.	*We **want** a reform.*
Ils **veulent vendre** leur maison.	*They **want to sell** their house.*
Je **voudrais** bien que tu me donnes des roses de ton jardin.	*I really **would like** you to give me some roses from your garden.*
Tu **en veux** combien?	*How many do you **want**?*
J'**en voudrais** quatre.	*I'**d like** four.*
Je peux t'en donner autant que tu **veux**.	*I can give you as many as you **wish**.*

En vouloir à

En vouloir means "to have a grudge against someone." The **en** here is part of the verb. So be careful when you see or hear a **en** with **vouloir**. It can lead to total misunderstanding.

Pourquoi tu lui **en veux**?	*Why do you **have a grudge against** him?*
Benoît **en veut à** son frère d'avoir fait échouer leurs projets.	*Benoît **holds it against** his brother that he made their projects fail.*
Ne m'**en veux** pas. Je ne l'ai pas fait exprès.	*Don't **hold it against** me. I did not do it on purpose.*
Tu ne m'**en veux** pas?	*No hard feelings?*

Envier/avoir envie de/avoir une envie de

They may look similar, but their meaning is quite different.

Envier

Je t'**envie**.	*I **envy** you.*
Denis vous **envie** de pouvoir faire ce voyage.	*Denis **envies** you for being able to take this trip.*

Avoir envie de

Nicolas **a envie de** s'installer à Menton.	*Nicolas **would like to** move to Menton.*
Qu'est-ce que vous **avez envie de** faire?	*What do you **feel like** doing?*
Loïc **avait** très **envie de** rire pendant la conférence.	*Loïc really **felt like** laughing during the conference.*
J'**ai envie de** toi.	*I **want** you.*

Avoir une envie de

Hélène, qui est enceinte, **a une envie** de chocolat.	*Hélène, who is pregnant, **has a craving** for chocolate.*
Gabriel **a des envies** subites de cornichons.	*Gabriel **has** sudden **cravings** for pickles.*

Attendre/s'attendre à

Attendre

Attendre can be followed by a direct object (notice there is no preposition before the object), an infinitive, or a dependent clause.

J'**attends** une livraison.	*I **am waiting** for a delivery.*
Nous **attendons** d'en savoir plus.	*We **are waiting** to know more about it.*
Ils **attendent** que vous preniez une décision.	*They **are waiting** for you to make a decision.*
J'**attends** votre réponse avec impatience.	*I'm **looking forward to** your answer.*
En attendant, je te souhaite bonne chance.	*Meanwhile, I wish you good luck.*

S'attendre à

When **attendre** is used in the pronominal form, it means *to expect*. It is followed by the preposition **à** and the subjunctive in a dependent clause.

Attendez-vous à des grèves!	*You **should expect** some strikes.*
Tu **t'attends** vraiment **à** ce qu'il dise la vérité?	*Do you really **expect** him to tell the truth?*
Paul **ne s'attendait pas à** gagner une médaille d'or.	*Paul **did not expect** to win a gold medal.*
Je **ne m'y attendais pas**.	*I **did not expect** it.*

EXERCICE
8·5

*Translate the following sentences, using inversion where needed and the **tu** or **vous** form, as indicated.*

1. They don't expect me to know how to play the piano.

   _____

2. Don't hold it against him! He is tired and he forgot the appointment. (**tu**)

   _____

3. I don't feel like going out tonight.

   _____

4. —I want to give you some oranges. How many do you want?—I want three. (**tu**)

   _____

5. I did not expect his reaction. I was so surprised.

   _____

6. I envy you. You are so lucky! (**vous**)

   _____

7. I'll wait for you in front of the statue of George Sand in the Luxembourg Garden. (**tu**)

_____

8. Marion does not talk to her brother. She holds a grudge against him. I don't know why.

_____

9. Charlotte has cravings for strawberries.

_____

10. I expect his victory in May.

_____

Manquer/manquer de/manquer à/il manque

The verb **manquer** (*to miss*) is a teacher's favorite when examination time comes. There are many rules to remember. Try and memorize some examples in context.

Manquer

First is **manquer** with a direct object, no preposition:

J'**ai manqué** le train à cause d'un accident dans le métro.	*I **missed** the train because of an accident in the subway.*
Bastien **a manqué** le cours d'informatique.	*Bastien **missed** the computer science course.*
Vous **avez manqué** Tara de cinq minutes.	*You **missed** Tara by five minutes.*
Le film était horrible. Vous **n'avez** rien **manqué**.	*The film was horrible. You **did not miss** anything.*
Marion **a manqué** une marche et elle est tombée.	*Marion **missed** a step and she fell.*

Manquer de

When the preposition **de** follows **manquer**, it means that something is lacking, insufficient, and sometimes weak.

Ce soufflé **manque de** goût. Tu as oublié d'ajouter de la noix de muscade?	*This soufflé **lacks** flavor. Did you forget to add some nutmeg?*
Odile **manque d'**imagination.	*Odile **lacks** imagination.*
Notre entreprise **manque de** main-d'œuvre.	*Our company **has a shortage of** labor.*
On **manque d'**air ici. Ouvrez les fenêtres!	*There **is no** air in here! Open the windows!*
Cette Adèle! Elle **ne manque pas d'audace**!	*That Adèle! She **has got some nerve**!*
Ne vous en faites pas! Ces enfants **ne manquent de rien**.	*Don't worry! These children **have everything they need**.*

Manquer à

When **manquer** is followed by the preposition **à**, the spectrum of meanings is quite impressive:

Tu me **manques**.	*I miss you.*

If you want to stay out of trouble, do not confuse:

Tu me **manques**.	*I miss you.*

with:

Je te **manque**?	*You miss me?*

Here are more examples:

Nous te **manquons**?	*Do you miss us?*
Leur ancien quartier leur **manque**.	*They miss their old neighborhood.*
Manuel te **manque** vraiment?	*Do you really miss Manuel?*
Manuel me **manque** terriblement.	*I miss Manuel terribly.*
Elle vous **manque**.	*You miss her.*
Vous me **manquez** tant.	*I miss you so much.*
Venise me **manque**.	*I miss Venice.*
Ses blagues nous **manquent**.	*We miss his jokes.*

To fail can be sometimes be translated with **manquer à**.

Valentin **a manqué à** ses devoirs.	*Valentin failed to do his duty.*
Vanessa **a manqué à** ses promesses.	*Vanessa failed to keep her word.*

Il manque

Il manque is an impersonal expression that takes on a lot of meanings.

Il manque deux pieds à la table.	*There are two legs missing from the table.*
Il leur manque 300 euros pour acheter cette chaise.	*They are short of 300 euros to buy this chair.*
Il ne manquait plus que ça!	*That's all we needed!*

EXERCICE

8·6

*Translate the following sentences, using the **est-ce que** form as needed and the **tu** or **vous** form, as indicated.*

1. Our organization is five thousand euros short of having a chance to win.

   _____

2. Édouard won't be here tonight. He missed his plane.

   _____

3. Andréa does not lack talent, but she is too shy.

   _____

4. I miss my grandmother Victorine.

   _____

5. Some pages are missing in this novel. That is strange . . .

_____

6. I am so sad. I missed Amélien by three minutes.

_____

7. Do you miss us? (**tu**)

_____

8. If you fail to do your duty, Clara will leave you. (**tu**)

_____

9. I miss our trips in Brittany.

_____

10. There are buttons missing on this cardigan.

_____

Savoir/connaître

You are aware of the verb **savoir** (*to know*), as the phrase *savoir faire* (*know-how*) is commonly used in English. However, you cannot learn **savoir** without becoming acquainted with the verb **connaître**, so that you can distinguish one from the other. **Connaître** means to know, to be acquainted with, and to be familiar with. In a figurative way, it means to enjoy, to live, and to experience. **Savoir** can be followed by a direct object or a dependent clause. It can also be translated in many ways.

Maryse **sait jouer** de la flûte.	Maryse **can play** the flute.
Eva **sait négocier** avec ses clients.	Eva **knows how to negotiate** with her clients.
Savez-vous où Éric habite?	Do you **know** where Éric lives?
Je **ne savais pas** qu'il était célibataire.	I **did not know** he was single.
Ça se **saurait** si c'était vrai.	People **would know** about it if it were true.
Elle **sait parler** aux ados.	She **is good at talking** to teenagers.
Savez-vous la nouvelle?	**Have** you **heard** the news?
Claire **sait écouter**.	Claire **is a good listener**.
Savoir, c'est pouvoir.	**Knowledge** is power.
Nous **savons bien** que le comptable est impliqué dans le complot.	We **are well aware** that the accountant is involved in the plot.

In many cases, *how* is used with *to know*. It is not used in French unless the speaker knows how something should be done and what needs to be emphasized.

Common usage:

Mon frère **sait changer** un pneu.	My brother **knows how to change** a tire.

Emphasis:

Je ne **sais vraiment pas comment** vous exprimer ma gratitude.	I **really don't know how** to express my gratitude.
Il **ne sait vraiment pas comment** expliquer ce qui s'est passé.	He **really does not know how** to explain what happened.

Connaître is always followed by a direct object. But it is never followed by a dependent clause. Remember, if you need a dependent clause with a conjunction after *to know*, don't think twice—**savoir** is the only answer.

Ils **connaissent** tous les musées de Lyon.	*They **know** all the museums in Lyon.*
Ma sœur **connaît** le rédacteur en chef du Monde.	*My sister **knows** the editor-in-chief of Le Monde.*
Elle l'**a connu** à la fac.	*She **met** him at the university.*
Sa bonté **ne connaît pas** de bornes.	*His/her kindness **knows no** limits.*
Bon nombre d'artistes **ont connu** la pauvreté.	*Many artists **have experienced** poverty.*
Il **a connu** la faim pendant son enfance.	*He **experienced** hunger during his youth.*
La Grèce **connaît** une grave crise économique.	*Greece **is going through** a serious economic crisis.*
Ils **ne connaissent pas** encore les coutumes de cette tribu.	*They **are not** yet **familiar with** the customs of this tribe.*

Savoir and **connaître** can be used together with an interesting nuance:

Savez-vous cette chanson?	*Do you **know** this song? (i.e., by heart)*
Connaissez-vous cette chanson?	*Do you **know** this song? (i.e., Are you familiar with it?)*

Savoir and pouvoir

Savoir is often used in French in contrast with **pouvoir**, depending on the meaning:

Tu **sais** nager?	***Can** you swim?*
Il ne **sait** pas lire.	*He **can't** read.*
Je **sais** nager mais je ne peux pas nager aujourd'hui car je suis enrhumé.	*I **can** swim, but I am not able to today because I have a cold.*
Il **sait** lire mais il ne peut pas lire maintenant car il a oublié ses lunettes.	*He **can** read, but he cannot read right now because he forgot his glasses.*

EXERCICE

8·7

*Translate the following sentences, using inversion as needed and the **tu** or **vous** form, as indicated.*

1. Do you know at what time they'll arrive? (**vous**)

   _____

2. Camille experienced hunger when she was young.

   _____

3. Can you drive? (**vous**)

   _____

4. I know she is always late.

   _____

5. The Langlois know how to organize a party.

_____

6. I am sure Jonas knows the truth.

_____

7. When will you know if we can visit them in Normandy? (**vous**)

_____

8. Véronique is going through a serious personal crisis.

_____

9. These children cannot even read. Please do something! (**vous**)

_____

10. Have you heard the news? (**tu**)

_____

EXERCICE
8·8

Match the two columns.

_____ 1. Claire a envie de	a. sa tante.
_____ 2. Tu ne peux pas t'imaginer à quel point	b. du piano.
_____ 3. Vanessa emprunte trop d'argent à	c. un miracle.
_____ 4. Ne vous attendez pas à	d. faire le tour du monde.
_____ 5. Louise ne sait pas vraiment jouer	e. tu me manques.

Using the infinitive

9

The causative form
The present participle
The gerund

Using the infinitive

A versatile verb form that can shorten a verbose sentence, the infinitive plays a role in several types of phrases containing more than one verb. If a sentence starts with a verb denoting a mode of perception, the second verb is in the infinitive. For example:

On entendait Martha **fredonner** une gavotte de Bach.	*We could hear Martha **humming** a gavotte by Bach.*
J'ai vu le chat **sauter** sur le manteau de la cheminée.	*I saw the cat **jumping** on mantelpiece.*
Nous écoutions la foule **crier**: « Vive le Roi! »	*We were listening to the crowd **shouting**: "Long live the King!"*
Patrick la regarde **écrire** son mémoire.	*Patrick watches her **writing** her thesis.*

The infinitive is used in expressions describing how one spends time. In English, the *-ing* form is used. In French, you need the preposition **à** + the verb in the infinitive:

Il passe son temps **à créer** des objets.	*He spends his time **creating** new objects.*
Monsieur Grandet passe son temps **à compter** son argent.	*Monsieur Grandet spends his time **counting** his money.*
Elle passe son temps **à rêver**.	*She spends her time **dreaming**.*
Le ministre de l'Agriculture passe son temps **à sillonner** la France.	*The minister of agriculture spends his time **traveling** all over France.*

EXERCICE
9·1

Translate the following sentences.

1. I saw Victorine eating a chocolate cake in her office.

_____

2. His cousin Grégoire spends his time playing basketball.

_____

3. My neighbor Carl spends his time watching television.

_____

4. I heard him talking in the hallway.

_____

5. Samuel spends his vacation visiting libraries in Paris.

_____

6. In the summer, we spend our time traveling in Europe.

_____

7. Carla saw him cutting wood in the garden.

_____

8. Laurent spends his time learning foreign languages.

_____

9. She heard them saying they would sell their house.

_____

10. I was watching him sleeping.

_____

The infinitive, followed by the preposition **à**, just like in the previous examples, also appears in expressions describing a person's physical posture during an activity:

Ils sont allongés **à regarder** les étoiles.	_They are lying down **watching** the stars._
Je suis debout **à attendre** le bus.	_I'm standing **waiting** for the bus._
Joanna est assise **à tricoter** une écharpe.	_Joanna is sitting **knitting** a scarf._
Il est appuyé contre la clôture **à regarder** les moutons.	_He is leaning against the fence **watching** the sheep._

EXERCICE
9·2

Match the two columns.

_____ 1. Tu es accroupi dans le jardin   a. à réfléchir à son destin.

_____ 2. Elle est étendue sur son lit   b. à boire une bière.

_____ 3. Ils sont accoudés au bar   c. à arracher les mauvaises herbes.

_____ 4. Elle est assise, la tête dans les mains
_____ 5. Vous êtes debout sur une chaise

d. à nettoyer les étagères de la bibliothèque.

e. à lire un roman d'amour.

EXERCICE
9·3

*Translate the following sentences, using the **tu** or **vous** form, as indicated.*

1. They are sitting in the grass watching the sunset.

   _____

2. The professor is standing reading a passage from *The Lover* by Marguerite Duras.

   _____

3. Xavier is lying on his bed reading the dictionary.

   _____

4. We are lying down on the sofa watching a new Italian film.

   _____

5. Yvon is squatting in the field picking some strawberries.

   _____

6. Édouard is leaning against the door of the refrigerator wondering what he is going to eat.

   _____

7. Lucien is leaning against the wall watching people dance.

   _____

8. You are standing on a chair cleaning the windows. (**vous**)

   _____

9. The novelist is sitting in front of her computer thinking about what she is going to write.

   _____

10. You are squatting in the kitchen trying to repair the door. (**tu**)

   _____

The causative form

When it is followed by the infinitive, the verb **faire** often expresses the idea of *having something done by someone* or of *causing something to happen*. This construction is called the causative form because the subject is identified as the ultimate cause of a particular action that may be performed by another subject. For example:

Je **nettoie** le sol.
Je **fais nettoyer** le sol.
Amélia **désinstalle** son antivirus.
Amélia **a fait désinstaller** son antivirus.
Alain **coupe** du bois.
Alain **fait couper** du bois.
Nous **décorons** la salle avec des ballons pour la célébration.
Nous **faisons décorer** la salle avec des ballons pour la célébration.

*I **clean** the floor.*
*I **have** the floor **cleaned**.*
*Amélia **is uninstalling** her antivirus software.*
*Amélia **had** her antivirus software **uninstalled**.*

*Alain **is cutting** some wood.*
*Alain **is having** some wood **cut**.*
*We **are decorating** the room with balloons for the celebration.*
*We **are having** the room **decorated** with balloons for the celebration.*

EXERCICE 9·4

Put the following sentences into the causative form. Pay attention to the tenses!

1. Je réparerai mon ordinateur.

   _____

2. Emmanuel remplacera toutes les lampes dans la bibliothèque.

   _____

3. J'ai visité les nouveaux bureaux de l'agence.

   _____

4. Shah Jahan a construit le Taj Mahal en mémoire de sa femme.

   _____

5. Envoie le paquet en express!

   _____

6. Victoria fera une robe pour le mariage de sa cousine.

   _____

7. Rédigez une demande de bourse de recherche!

   _____

8. Il livrera les fleurs à Madame de Guermantes avant midi.

   _____

9. Vous corrigerez les fautes d'orthographe dans votre essai.

_____

10. Raphaël a lavé sa voiture avant de partir en vacances.

_____

The present participle

You have seen and used the **participe passé** (*past participle*) many times in compound tenses, such as the **passé composé**. The **participe présent** (*present participle*) plays a different role in French syntax, often as a convenient substitute for nouns, verbs, and other parts of speech, for the sake of concision.

> La jeune femme qui chante dans le chœur est ma nièce.
>
> *The young woman who sings in the choir is my niece.*

A present participle may make this sentence shorter—and more elegant. It depends on the context and the flow of the sentence:

> La jeune fille **chantant** dans le chœur est ma nièce.

To form this participle, we must drop the **-ons** ending from the **nous** form in the present tense and add **-ant**.

arriver	*to arrive*		
nous arrivons	*we arrive*	arrivant	*arriving*
agir	*to act*		
nous agissons	*we act*	agissant	*acting*
attendre	*to wait*		
nous attendons	*we wait*	attendant	*waiting*
prendre	*to take*		
nous prenons	*we take*	prenant	*taking*
connaître	*to know*		
nous connaissons	*we know*	connaissant	*knowing*
rire	*to laugh*		
nous rions	*we laugh*	riant	*laughing*
concevoir	*to design*		
nous concevons	*we design*	concevant	*designing*

Some spelling changes occur with some **-cer** and **-ger** verbs. Note the added **-e-** in **nous bougeons** and **bougeant**. This spelling is introduced in order to maintain the "soft" pronunciation of the sound represented by the letter **g**. In **nous finançons**, it is the **cédille** that keeps the **c** soft. **NOTE:** Remember: **a, o, u** → hard sound; **e, i** → soft sound.

Let's first look at verbs that require an extra -e-:

bouger	*to move*		
nous bougeons	*we move*	bougeant	*moving*
ranger	*to put away*		
nous rangeons	*we put away*	rangeant	*putting away*
manger	*to eat*		
nous mangeons	*we eat*	mangeant	*eating*
obliger	*to force*		
nous obligeons	*we force*	obligeant	*forcing*

And let's look at the verbs requiring a **cédille**:

avancer	*to advance*		
nous avançons	*we advance*	avançant	*advancing*
financer	*to finance*		
nous finançons	*we finance*	finançant	*financing*
effacer	*to erase*		
nous effaçons	*we erase*	effaçant	*erasing*
dédicacer	*to autograph*		
nous dédicaçons	*we autograph*	dédicaçant	*autographing*

Three verbs have an irregular present participle:

être	*to be*	étant	*being*
avoir	*to have*	ayant	*having*
savoir	*to know*	sachant	*knowing*

Pronominal verbs can also be used in the **participe présent**. Do not forget the pronoun corresponding to the subject. Let's look at the present participle of **se laver** (*to wash oneself*):

me lavant	*washing myself*
te lavant	*washing yourself*
se lavant	*washing himself/herself*
nous lavant	*washing ourselves*
vous lavant	*washing yourselves*
se lavant	*washing themselves*

Étant opposée à cette nouvelle politique sociale, elle a démissionné.	***Being*** *opposed to this new social policy, she resigned.*
Sachant qu'il allait échouer, il a tout abandonné.	***Knowing*** *he was going to fail, he gave everything up.*
J'ai croisé Nathalie en me **promenant** dans le parc Georges Brassens.	*I ran into Nathalie while **strolling** in the Georges Brassens Park.*
Il a fait tomber la boîte en se **penchant** par la fenêtre.	*He dropped the box while **leaning** out of the window.*
Ayant randonné pendant des heures, Julie est rentrée épuisée.	*After **hiking** for hours, Julie came back exhausted.*

Using the present participle

Sometimes when a certain action or activity is associated with a person, the present participle can function as a noun. In this case, the present participle behaves like a noun, respecting the rules of agreement in gender and number.

un débutant	*a beginner (m.)*	**une débutante**	*a beginner (f.)*
un passant	*a passerby (m.)*	**une passante**	*a passerby (f.)*

Many **participes présent** can also function as adjectives. They are called **adjectifs verbaux**. In that case, the **participe présent** agrees with the noun it modifies:

une odeur **alléchante**	*a tempting smell*
une situation **hilarante**	*a hilarious situation*
un argument **convaincant**	*a convincing argument*
un voyage **fatigant**	*a tiring trip*

The **participe présent** can also be used in a causal clause, in conjunction with the past participle and followed by **que**. Explaining the cause of an action, this type of dependent clause may also be introduced by words such as **parce que** and **puisque**.

Puisque tu ne veux pas m'accompagner, je vais chez Maria tout seul.	*Since you don't want to come along, I'm going to Maria's on my own.*
Étant donné que tu ne veux pas m'accompagner, je vais chez Maria tout seul.	*Since you don't want to come along, I'm going to Maria's on my own.*

In the preceding sentence, the present participle of the verb **être** is used in conjunction with the past participle of the verb **donner**. In this construction, both participles are invariable.

Here are some other examples of uses of the **participe présent**:

Ayant été absent lors de la réunion, tu lis le compte rendu.	*Since you were absent from the meeting, you are reading the report.*
Sachant qu'il n'aurait aucune chance de gagner, il a refusé de jouer aux cartes.	*Knowing he had no chance of winning, he refused to play cards.*
Ayant conscience du danger, Rémi a été très prudent.	*Being aware of the danger, Rémi was very cautious.*
S'étant fracturé le poignet, Quentin a dû se retirer de la compétition.	*Having fractured his wrist, Quentin had to withdraw from the competition.*
Ayant lu tout le roman, Lucie pouvait répondre à toutes les questions.	*Having read the whole novel, Lucie could answer all the questions.*

The gerund

The gerund, which is called **gérondif** in French, tells us how two actions are connected, often specifying manner, circumstances, causality, and time sequence. In many cases, the two actions are simultaneous. The gerund is formed by placing the particle **en** in front of a present participle.

Anthony s'est cassé le bras **en faisant** du ski.	*Anthony broke his arm **while skiing**.*
Appoline chantait **en conduisant**.	*Appoline was singing **while driving**.*
Clément est devenu célèbre **en créant** ses propres sites web.	*Clement became famous **by creating** his own websites.*
Ils se sont enrichis **en spéculant** à la Bourse de Paris.	*They got rich **by speculating** on the Paris Stock Exchange.*

When **tout** precedes the gerund, it underscores a tension, a contradiction between two actions:

Tout en étant un bon élève, Mathis est paresseux.

While being a good student, Mathis is lazy.

Tout en critiquant les magazines féminins, Tatiana achetait tous les numéros.

While criticizing the women's magazines, Tatiana bought every issue.

Tout en pleurant, Damien riait.

While crying, Damien was laughing.

Tout en prétendant être de notre côté, son comportement était discutable.

While claiming he was on our side, he behaved in a questionable way.

EXERCICE
9·5

Complete with the proper verb form.

1. Ce chef célèbre boit toujours un verre de vin en (faire) _____ la cuisine.

2. Laura a gagné la compétition en (nager) _____ encore plus vite.

3. Ce n'est pas en (regarder) _____ la télé que tu vas perdre du poids!

4. Nous nous arrêterons à Sarlat en (descendre) _____ dans le Roussillon.

5. (Accepter) _____ leur défaite avec élégance hier soir, les nageurs ont été salués par le public.

6. (Ignorer) _____ tout de la situation, elle vient de faire une gaffe monumentale.

7. Comment Martha a-t-elle pu gagner tant d'argent?—En (investir) _____ sagement.

8. (Être) _____ de gauche, elle ne pouvait pas voter pour ce candidat même s'il lui plaisait.

9. Tout en (faire semblant) _____ de dormir, Jean écoutait la conversation de ses parents.

10. Il ne se souvenait plus si Élisabeth préférait l'or ou l'argent en (choisir) _____ une bague.

EXERCICE
9·6

*Translate the following sentences, using inversion as needed and the **tu** or **vous** form, as indicated.*

1. I work while listening to classical music.

_____

2. We were talking politics while we were preparing dinner.

_____

3. While being nice to her, Paul always said nasty things behind her back.

_____

4. This trip was too tiring. We spent our time carrying suitcases from one place to the other.

   _____

5. Knowing Henri was a dangerous man, Loïc talked about it to his boss.

   _____

6. Having won a lot of money at the lottery, they decided to travel in Asia.

   _____

7. Your ideas are not convincing enough.

   _____

8. Andréa lost her keys while playing frisbee on the beach.

   _____

9. While criticizing this writer, she used to buy all his books.

   _____

10. He was knitting a sweater while watching a soccer game.

    _____

 # Verbs and prepositions

When a verb is followed by another verb in the infinitive, the first thing to ask yourself is whether or not there is a preposition between them. In sentences based on the pattern of **j'aime lire** (*I like to read*), this is a question of life and death: many French sentences, which follow the same pattern, insist on inserting a preposition between the two verbs, so the preposition precedes the infinitive. All this comes naturally to the French, who don't even wonder why it's necessary to say, **Je songe à prendre ma retraite** (*I'm thinking of retiring*).

Things are simpler in English because the only preposition we need to worry about is *to*, which functions as an infinitive marker. For example, if a verb is standing alone, we have no idea of its form, because modern English does not have an infinitive ending. For all practical purposes, it's just a word. On the other hand, *to read* and *to write* are infinitives. In French, when we write the word **parler**, we know it's an infinitive, because we recognize the infinitive ending -**er**.

So how do we learn when to drop the preposition and how to choose among **de**, **à**, **sur**, and so on? While we wait for some genius to discover a magic formula, we can take advantage of a mnemonic technique, which has helped us learn the correct gender of a noun. When you learned the word *moon*, you memorized it as **la lune**, not just **lune**. So when you form a mental image of a particular infinitive that isn't followed by a preposition, you can visualize it followed by a "zero"—for example, **parler**. You will then know that **Je veux lire** is correct!

When you run into verbs that must be followed by a preposition, look for patterns, and memorize them, according to preposition, always forming a unit consisting of a verb and its preposition. Imagine you're learning the verb **apprendre**. If you memorize it as **apprendre à**, you will always use the correct preposition.

Verbs not followed by a preposition

Let's start with verbs that are *not* followed by a preposition:

aimer	*to like, to love*
aller	*to go*
avouer	*to admit*
compter	*to intend, to plan*
désirer	*to desire, to wish*
détester	*to hate (to)*
devoir	*must, to have to*
écouter	*to listen to*

espérer	*to hope to*
faire	*to do*
falloir	*must, to be necessary to*
laisser	*to let, to allow*
oser	*to dare (to)*
paraître	*to appear, to seem*
penser	*to think*
pouvoir	*can, to be able to*
préférer	*to prefer*
prétendre	*to claim*
savoir	*to know (how to)*
sembler	*to seem to*
sentir	*to feel, to think*
souhaiter	*to wish to*
venir	*to come*
voir	*to see*
vouloir	*to want to*

Nous **allons skier** tous les hivers.	*We **go skiing** every winter.*
Ludivine **souhaite partir** en Argentine.	*Ludivine **wishes to travel** to Argentina.*
Je **n'ose pas demander** à Benoît de m'aider.	*I **don't dare ask** Benoît to help me.*
Préfères-tu aller chez Ludovic sans nous?	*Do you **prefer going** to Ludovic's without us?*
Il faut démolir ce vieux bâtiment, sinon il va s'effondrer.	*This old building **must be demolished**, otherwise it is going to collapse.*
Viens voir!	*Come take a look!*

Note the single subject in the preceding examples: these sentences exemplify the subject–indicative verb–infinitive verb pattern. In fact, the infinitive comes in handy when we need to avoid repeating the same subject. For example, one may say in improper French: **Je pense que je suis en mesure de le faire** (*I think I can do it*). But saying **Je pense être en mesure de le faire** not only is more elegant but also is correct French.

Let's see what happens when there are two subjects. Remember, we are still discussing sentences based on the subject–indicative verb–infinitive verb pattern. With one subject, we can get away with a simple sentence. When there are two subjects, we need to create a complex sentence and introduce the dependent clause with **que**. The verb in the main clause will determine the mood (indicative or subjunctive) of the verb in the dependent clause.

Ils préfèrent oublier cette sale histoire.	*They prefer to forget this nasty story.*
Ils préfèrent **qu'elle oublie** cette sale histoire.	*They prefer her to forget this nasty story.*
Tu détestes être en retard.	*You hate being late.*
Tu détestes **que je sois** en retard.	*You hate me being late.*

Remember that there are many zero-preposition verbs in French whose English equivalents require a preposition, and vice versa.

Colombe cherche un livre d'Ananda Devi.	*Colombe is looking **for** a book by Ananda Devi.*
Regarde l'arc-en-ciel!	*Look **at** the rainbow!*
Maxence n'a pas répondu **aux** critiques.	*Maxence didn't answer the critics.*
J'ai permis **aux** enfants de regarder un film de kung-fu.	*I let the children watch a kung fu movie.*

Choose the right verb in the following list to complete each sentence.

aimez	désirent	a détesté	devons	laisse
pensent	pourrais	sembles	viendra	voudrais

1. Candice _____ toujours _____ faire le ménage.

2. Tu _____ angoissé par la présence du directeur.

3. Je _____ devenir chorégraphe.

4. Vous _____ enseigner le dessin aux enfants.

5. Est-ce qu' Émilie _____ au rendez-vous qu'elle m'a fixé ?

6. Faustin et Aimée _____ ardemment avoir un enfant.

7. _____-la prendre ses décisions elle-même !

8. _____-tu me prêter ton enregisteur numérique ?

9. Nous _____ écrire un livre sur le subjonctif en français.

10. Elles _____ que le juge est corrompu.

Verbs followed by the preposition à

Sometimes, although rarely, even native French speakers have to refresh their memory when it comes to **à** verbs and **de** verbs. Clearly, we are dealing with a fundamental dichotomy. As mentioned previously, a verb and its appropriate preposition should be memorized as a unit.

aider à	*to help to*
s'amuser à	*to enjoy*
apprendre à	*to learn to, to show how to*
arriver à	*to manage to*
aspirer à	*to aspire to*
s'attendre à	*to expect to*
autoriser à	*to authorize to*
avoir à	*to have to*
chercher à	*to try to, to attempt to*
commencer à	*to start to*
consentir à	*to agree to, to consent to*
continuer à	*to continue to, to keep on*
se décider à	*to make up one's mind to*
encourager à	*to encourage to*
se faire à	*to get used to*
faire attention à	*to pay attention to*
s'habituer à	*to get used to*
hésiter à	*to hesitate to*
inciter à	*to encourage to*
s'intéresser à	*to get interested in*
inviter à	*to invite to*

se joindre à	*to join*
se mettre à	*to start to, to begin to*
parvenir à	*to manage to*
préparer à (se)	*to get ready to*
renoncer à	*to give up*
se résigner à	*to resign oneself to*
réussir à	*to succeed in*
songer à	*to think about*
tenir à	*to want, to insist on, to be eager to*
viser à	*to aim at*

Maria apprend **à** monter à cheval.	*Maria is learning how to ride a horse.*
Nous les avons invités **à** prendre un verre.	*We invited them to have a drink.*
Le président du conseil d'administration tient **à** vous voir cet après-midi.	*The president of the board wants to see you this afternoon.*
Nous ne sommes pas parvenus **à** le convaincre **d**'inviter Laura **à** se joindre à nous.	*We did not manage to convince him to invite Laura to join us.*

EXERCICE
10·2

Match the two columns.

_____ 1. Ils pensent a. au progrès de la science.

_____ 2. Je pense b. en son fils aîné.

_____ 3. Cet universitaire croit c. à leurs prochaines vacances.

_____ 4. Elle croit d. il y a trop de risques.

_____ 5. Nous pensons que e. les inviter à devenir membres de notre club.

Verbs followed by the preposition de

While you're memorizing these verbs, try not to use this particular preposition as a crutch. French teachers have noticed that students sometimes imagine that **de** is a generic preposition that will do when they draw a blank. For example, the sentence **J'aime de lire** is many a French teacher's nightmare. It is important, therefore, to remember that the **à/de** divide must never be ignored.

accepter de	*to accept, to agree to*
accuser de	*to accuse (of)*
s'arrêter de	*to stop*
avoir besoin de	*to need to*
avoir envie de	*to feel like, to want*
avoir l'intention de	*to intend to*
avoir peur de	*to be afraid of*
cesser de	*to stop, to cease*
choisir de	*to choose to*
conseiller de	*to advise (to)*

se contenter de	*to content oneself with*
convaincre de	*to convince (to)*
craindre de	*to fear (to)*
défendre de	*to forbid (to)*
demander de	*to ask (to)*
se dépêcher de	*to hurry to*
s'efforcer de	*to try hard to*
empêcher de	*to prevent (from)*
s'empêcher de	*to refrain from*
envisager de	*to contemplate*
essayer de	*to try to*
éviter de	*to avoid*
s'excuser de	*to apologize for*
faire semblant de	*to pretend to*
feindre de	*to feign to, to pretend to*
finir de	*to finish, to end up*
interdire de	*to forbid (to)*
menacer de	*to threaten to*
mériter de	*to deserve to*
offrir de	*to offer to*
oublier de	*to forget to*
parler à	*to speak to*
parler de	*to speak about*
permettre de	*to allow (to), to permit (to)*
persuader de	*to persuade (to), to convince (to)*
se plaindre de	*to complain of*
projeter de	*to plan to/on*
promettre de	*to promise to*
refuser de	*to refuse to*
regretter de	*to regret*
remercier de	*to thank (for)*
reprocher de	*to reproach for*
soupçonner de	*to suspect of*
se souvenir de	*to remember to*
tâcher de	*to try to*

Vincent a accepté **de** participer **à** l'événement.	*Vincent has accepted to attend the event.*
J'ai conseillé **à** Élise **d'**aller voir un avocat.	*I advised Élise to see a lawyer.*
Florent se plaint toujours **d'**avoir trop de travail.	*Florent always complains about having too much work.*
Stéphanie a refusé **de** lui révéler le secret.	*Stéphanie refused to reveal the secret to him/her.*

Did you know that prepositions can be glamorous? In World War II, Dutch resistance fighters had no problem catching German spies, because there are certain place names that foreigners, even fluent Dutch speakers, regularly mispronounce. A spy trying to pass as a native French speaker better watch his or her prepositions, for an incorrect preposition can derail not only an otherwise elegant speech in French, but perhaps a career as well. For example, let us imagine a meeting of European business executives, taking place in July, during which an independent contractor, ostensibly from France, describes himself as more efficient than any of his competitors. No doubt in his mind that he should be awarded the lucrative contract for a project that is to be launched in October. Listen to the conclusion of his pitch: **Je peux le faire dans quatre semaines**.

Before he could finish his sentence, he was asked to leave. What went wrong? Well, a Francophone member of the group immediately noticed that the "French" entrepreneur used the wrong preposition. He obviously wanted to say, *It would take me four weeks to finish the job*, but what he actually said was *I can finish that job in four weeks*, which made no sense, because the job was supposed to start in October. Had he learned the correct preposition, he would have said: **Je peux le faire en quatre semaines**, or *It would take me four weeks to finish the job*, and that would not have aroused any suspicion.

Having fun with prepositions

On the other end of the knowledge spectrum, here's a witty letter, written by a student of mine, who not only knows her grammar, but also composes her missive as a charming bouquet of colorful prepositions, homonyms, and *faux amis*.

> Les prépositions caméléonesques et capricieuses
> Ma chère petite-fille Chloé,

Je t'applaudis! Je suis ravie **d'**apprendre que tu as l'intention **de** faire une maîtrise de Lettres à New York University. Lorsque tu commenceras **à** apprendre la langue de Voltaire, tu tomberas amoureuse **de** la belle littérature française. Mais il faut faire attention: on dit que la grammaire, c'est *une chanson douce*—je paraphrase le titre d'un livre célèbre d'Érik Orsenna. Moi, je dis qu'elle est parsemée **de** mystères, hérissée **de** pièges et épicée **de** magie!

Par exemple, quelques prépositions sont des sorcières, de vrais caméléons, qui ont le pouvoir de métamorphoser le sens d'un verbe. Voici quelques exemples:

de/par: Je fêterai mon prochain anniversaire **dans** la vallée de Napa, entourée **de** ma tribu californienne. Madame Obama y fêtera son prochain anniversaire, comme moi, entourée **de** sa tribu et aussi **par** le Secret Service—la sauvegarde contre un éventuel danger.

de/à/par: Elle tient sa petite-fille **par** la main; la petite tient **d'**elle le bleu de ses yeux, le blond platine de ses cheveux; bouquinovore et francophile, elle tient **à** sa collection de livres français, de Gustave Flaubert **à** Amélie Nothomb.

Il y a un mec que je connais qui est vraiment agaçant, **ennuyeux** et **ennuyant**. Il n'a pas le droit **de** tutoyer LÉO, mon chaton chéri; il n'a pas droit **à** cette forme d'adresse—(c'est différent si *droit* est suivi **d'**un nom ou **d'**un verbe). Une princesse ne peut jamais échapper **à** sa cage dorée; Charles Manson ne pourra jamais s'échapper **de** prison (figuratif ou littéral).

dans/en (général/spécifique; temps): D'habitude, les vedettes volent **en** jet privé; moi, je suis **dans** l'avion **à** destination **de** Paris, j'étudie *French Demystified* par Annie Heminway; je dois maîtriser les pièges et les défis de la langue française **avant** l'atterrissage. **En** deux heures, j'ai lu le « Chapitre 14: All About Prepositions ». **Dans** quatre heures, je serai **à** Paris, les prépositions peaufinées!

Il y a des prépositions capricieuses qui flirtent avec les verbes, sans formule:

de/en: Jeanne Gonzalès éclata **en** sanglots quand elle vit le portrait de Berthe Morisot par Édouard Manet; elle écumait **de** rage et elle fondit **en** larmes. Sa rivale éclata-t-elle **de** rire, ou riait-t-elle **aux** éclats ou **jusqu'**aux larmes lorsqu'elle décortiqua ce portrait?

de/au: La mère d'Édouard Manet adore jouer **du** piano; pianoter; elle s'évade **de** la vie quotidienne; elle n'a aucune envie **de** jouer **au** golf, un passe-temps inutile, **à** son avis.

Les verbes s'amusent aussi bien que les prépositions; sans règle:

Gervaise, la blanchisseuse de Zola, s'occupe **de** tout: elle **fait** la vaisselle, elle **fait** la lessive et elle **lave** le linge au lavoir. À noter, c'est le **blanchissage**, ce n'est pas le **blanchiment** d'argent.

Je **jette** un coup d'œil **à** la garde-robe de notre cher écrivain, Alain Mabanckou, et je lui **fais** un clin d'œil.

Et les verbes qui trafiquent avec leurs prépositions:

Avoir les pieds **sur** terre: si jamais un tremblement **de** terre vous frappe, vous tombez **à** terre; on n'a pas envie **de** vous mettre **en** terre; on se flanque **par** terre; on veut rentrer **sous** terre (de honte); ne pas toucher terre.

Le sens d'un verbe peut changer selon la présentation d'un pronom réfléchi:

Eva Gonzalès, élève de Manet, peintre célèbre, **éclipse** sa sœur cadette Jeanne; tout à coup, juste après la mort du maître, elle **s'éclipse** et décède.

On se **met à** nu, comme Ananda Devi; on **est nu** comme un ver, comme Amélie Nothomb à Burning Man.

On ne peut pas négliger la position des adjectifs; avant ou après le nom—figuratif ou littéral.

Charles de Gaulle était de grande taille. C'était un homme **grand**—il mesurait 1,93 mètre. En période de crise, il a vraiment été un **grand** homme. Il restera dans les annales de l'Histoire.

Et les accents, le circonflexe, par exemple?

Elle revient de son séjour à l'Île de Ré **hâlée**; les marins ont **halé** une grosse baleine à bord.

Et les homonymes, féminin ou masculin? Et les homonymes euphoriques?

En face de **son poêle à** bois, mon fils cadet Guillaume trouve un **poil** de son chat Aphrodite dans **la poêle** à **galettes**, ce n'est pas marrant.

J'en ai marre: je me cache **sous un voile** et je mets **les voiles** (f.)

En **vers**, elle écrit la vie d'un **ver vert** qui se trouve dans un **verre** de rosé à Ver-sur-Mer.

Chez moi, à la campagne, le terrain est couvert **de pins**, le panier est rempli **de pain**.

Érik Orsenna me dit que la **mer** est sa **mère** pas son **maire**.

Ça suffit! J'espère que mes conseils n'ont pas gâché ton appétit pour les études du français!

Bon courage, ma petite-fille chérie!

Je t'embrasse très fort, Lili

Lisa Ehrenkranz
(*See* Translations *in the back of this book for English version of letter.*)

EXERCICE
10·3

Complete with a preposition if necessary.

1. Nous vous remercions vivement _____ être venus si nombreux.

2. L'ambassadeur voudrait _____ éviter _____ provoquer une crise diplomatique.

3. J'ai besoin _____ acheter un nouveau climatiseur. Tu peux m'aider _____ en choisir un?

4. Pourquoi hésites-tu _____ le contacter?

5. Mon beau-père a l'intention _____ investir dans l'or.

6. Je doute qu'il accepte _____ signer un contrat de mariage.

7. Le directeur tient _____ vous parler immédiatement!

8. Je te promets, je vais essayer _____ apprendre tous ces verbes par cœur.

9. Philippe est très timide. Il n'ose pas _____ contredire ses collègues de bureau.

10. Je n'ai pas pu m'empêcher _____ rire quand il a fait son discours.

11. L'éditeur de Claire s'attend _____ recevoir des critiques favorables à la parution de son livre.

12. N'oublie pas _____ prendre de l'essence. Le réservoir est presque vide.

13. Le syndicat menace _____ faire grève si les conditions ne s'améliorent pas.

14. Le nouveau ministre de l'Éducation voudrait _____ « mieux payer » les professeurs.

15. Est-ce que tu te souviens _____ l'année la naissance de Julien?

16. Quand commencerez-vous _____ travailler chez Guerlain?

17. Dépêche-toi _____ finir tes devoirs. Je voudrais _____ sortir prendre l'air.

18. Il faut _____ comparer les deux propositions.

19. Édouard ne peut pas s'habituer _____ son nouvel emploi.

20. Fabien m'a encouragé _____ suivre des cours en ligne.

EXERCICE
10·4

*Translate the following sentences, using the **tu** or **vous** form, as indicated.*

1. José and Julie invited us to spend our vacation with them.

   _____

2. We are going to buy a new computer.

   _____

3. Joël hates to cook.

   _____

4. Sophie cannot get used to getting up at 6 A.M. every morning.

   _____

5. They managed to meet the president of Air France.

   _____

6. I suspect him of pretending to be sick this weekend.

   _____

7. Nicolas is afraid he will lose the elections.

   _____

8. They promised to visit us at the end of the month.

   _____

9. You have to learn how to play the guitar. (**tu**)

_____

10. I hope you like your new apartment.

_____

_____

Restore the missing prepositions in front of nouns or verbs, when necessary.
(See Translations *in the back of this book for the English.)*

Port-au-Prince
     Je suis né à Port-au-Prince en Haïti, j'ai grandi et passé mon enfance à Petit-Goâve. **À**
Port-au-Prince, j'ai travaillé comme journaliste, puis j'ai dû quitté mon pays, exilé, pour venir **à**
Montréal où j'ai travaillé **à** l'usine, **dans** différentes usines **avant** d'écrire mon premier roman.

     Montréal à écrire
     C'est au Carré Saint-Louis que j'ai commencé _____ écrire. Pour moi, Montréal,
c'est la machine _____ écrire. C'est la modernité. Je n'ai jamais cru que je pourrais
écrire _____ la main _____ Montréal. Montréal, c'est aussi la distance.
Je suis _____ cette petite chambre et j'écris _____ Petit-Goâve, Port-au-Prince
tout en sachant que les gens qui vont me lire, pour la plupart, ne connaissent pas ces villes. Ça
me donne une certaine liberté. Je n'ai pas _____ fictionaliser ces villes. Elles sont déjà
fictions pour mes lecteurs.

     Ville en images
     Quand j'ai fait un film _____ Montréal, j'ai voulu que ce soit _____ hiver.
Un hiver aussi fort que l'été du tournage de *Comment faire l'amour*. Parce que je trouvais que
c'était comme si je regardais Montréal cette fois-ci pour lui-même, pour elle-même. Et _____
Montréal, il y a un hiver. Je ne peux pas _____ passer ma vie _____ croire que
Montréal est une ville du Sud. Montréal, c'est aussi une ville nordique. J'ai voulu m'approcher _____
cet hiver-là et essayer _____ l'apprivoiser, essayer _____ sentir cela parce que
je crois que c'est l'image fondamentale de Montréal et du Québec. D'ailleurs Gilles Vigneault, le
grand poète québécois a dit: « D'un glaçon, j'ai fait l'hiver. Mon pays, ce n'est pas un pays, c'est
l'hiver ». Je ne peux pas continuer _____ ne pas voir qu'il y a un hiver dans ce pays, et
j'ai voulu qu'il soit le plus fort. Et dans « Comment conquérir l'Amérique _____ une nuit »,
il me semblait que je devais _____ faire quelque chose qui réconcilie les deux villes et
Montréal et Port-au-Prince, deux villes qui m'habitent. J'ai pensé qu'il faudrait qu'un film
montre un peu les passages successifs entre les deux villes comme s'il n'y avait même pas
d'espace. Je parle _____ l'espace tendre _____ Montréal et Port-au-Prince.
Donc c'était un plaisir que je voulais me faire, de faire ce film. J'ai pas été surpris _____
la ville. Je voulais que l'image me fasse voir la ville sous un autre angle, d'une autre manière, et
ça je l'ai voulu. Oui, tout à fait. Et je l'ai eu. J'ai voulu aussi qu'il y ait des choses que l'être
humain ne peut pas _____ voir. C'est trop minuscule, on y passe . . . On voit la ville
tellement avec nos émotions quand on y passe et que je me suis dit que peut-être je, en
regardant _____ le film, je regarderai _____ les choses que je n'ai pas vues
parce que je les avais tellement absorbées rapidement en émotion et non en images.

     Un petit tour de ville et puis s'ennuie
     Je ne regarde pas _____ les villes précisément. Une grande majorité de mes
chroniques à l'étranger se passent _____ une salle de bain ou _____ une
chambre d'hôtel. Mon rêve, c'est de ne jamais être un touriste. Le touriste pour moi, c'est celui

qui regarde, qui cherche à savoir. Moi, je ne cherche pas _____ savoir. Je cherche à sentir. Il me faut un but. Je marche, je vais _____ un copain dans une ville que je viens à peine _____ connaître. C'est le trajet qui m'intéresse et le désir _____ être chez le copain. C'est beaucoup plus les intérieurs qui me plaisent, être _____ un bar, être _____ une libraire, être _____ un ami, être un peu partout. Le trajet, quand je vais dans une ville généralement—comme j'y vais comme conférencier et pour mes livres—je suis reçu par quelqu'un et qui me fait toujours faire un petit tour de la ville. C'est la partie la moins agréable pour moi parce que je n'aime pas qu'on me raconte une ville et son histoire. Et je n'aime pas qu'on me montre surtout les monuments ou les endroits importants. Ce qui m'intéresse, c'est juste _____ marcher et _____ voir le peu possible qui arrive _____ attirer ma rétine. Et finalement—incubation, _____ finir—sentir la ville. Je veux que la ville s'amène _____ moi. Je ne veux pas la découvrir. Je veux qu'elle me découvre.

Extrait d'un entretien de Dany Laferrière réalisé par Annie Heminway à Montréal en février 2009, pour blog *La ville est ailleurs*, aubepine.blog.lemonde.fr de Frédéric Antoine Brosson et Annie Heminway.

A final thought

Allow me to reinforce the mantra of this chapter—watch your prepositions!—by imagining a rather catastrophic misunderstanding that highlights the perils of ignorance. A cautionary tale for the prepositionally challenged.

> Louise: Lucas, je t'**en** veux terriblement d'avoir offert un si joli cadeau à Lola.
> Lucas: Eh bien, comme tu me veux malgré cette gaffe, *tout est pour le mieux dans le meilleur des mondes possibles.*

Bonne chance à toutes et à tous!

Translations

2

Strait Is the Gate

André Gide, 1909

"Why," said she, "wasn't the door shut?"

"I knocked, but you didn't answer. Alissa, you know I'm going tomorrow?"

She answered nothing, but I laid down the necklace, which she could not succeed in fastening. The word *engagement* seemed to me too bare, too brutal; I used I know not what periphrasis in its stead. As soon as Alissa understood what I meant, I thought I saw her sway and lean against the mantelpiece for support—but I myself was trembling so much that in my fearfulness, I avoided looking at her.

I was near her, and without raising my eyes, I took her hand; she did not free herself, but bending down her face a little and raising my hand a little, she put her lips on it and murmured, as she half leant against me:

"No, Jerome, no; don't, please, let us be engaged."

"Why?"

"It's I that ought to ask you why," she said, "why change?"

I did not dare speak to her of yesterday's conversation, but no doubt she felt I was thinking of it, and as if in answer to my thought, said, as she looked at me earnestly:

"You are wrong, dear. I do not need so much happiness. Are we not happy enough as we are?"

She tried in vain to smile.

"No, since I have to leave you."

"Listen, Jerome, I can't speak to you this evening—don't let's spoil our last minutes. No, no. I'm as fond of you as ever; don't be afraid. I'll write to you; I'll explain. I promise I'll write to you—tomorrow—as soon as you have gone. Leave me now!"

5

The Magic Skin

Honoré de Balzac, 1831

When I was alone with her, I had not a word to say, or if I did speak, I renounced love; and I affected gaiety but ill, like a courtier who has a bitter mortification to hide. I tried in every way to make myself indispensable in her life, and necessary to her vanity and to her comfort; I was a plaything at her pleasure, a slave always at her side. And when I had frittered away the day in this way, I went back to my work at night, securing merely two or three hours' sleep in the early morning.

But I had not, like Rastignac, the "English system" at my fingertips, and I very soon saw myself without a penny. I fell at once into that precarious way of life which industriously hides cold and miserable depths beneath an elusive surface of luxury; I was a coxcomb without conquests, a penniless fop, a nameless gallant. The old sufferings were renewed, but less sharply; no doubt I was growing used to the painful crisis. Very often my sole diet consisted of the scanty provision of cakes and tea that is offered in drawing-rooms, or one of the countess's great dinners must sustain me for two whole days. I used all my time, and exerted every effort and all my powers of observation, to penetrate the impenetrable character of Fœdora. Alternate hope and despair had swayed my opinions; for me she was sometimes the tenderest, sometimes the most unfeeling of women. But these transitions from joy to sadness became unendurable; I sought to end the horrible conflict within me by extinguishing love.

10

Translation of letter

My dear granddaughter Chloé,

I commend you! I am delighted to learn that you plan to pursue a master's degree in literature at New York University. Once you begin to learn Voltaire's language, you will fall in love with the beauty of French literature. But be careful: they say that grammar is *a sweet song*–I paraphrase the title of a well-known book by the French author Érik Orsenna, I say that it is riddled with mystery, bristling with pitfalls, and spiced with magic!

For example, some prepositions are wizards, chameleons, able to completely transform the meaning of a verb. Here are a few examples:

de/par: I will celebrate my next birthday in Napa Valley, surrounded by my California clan. Mrs. Obama will celebrate her next birthday there, like me, surrounded by her clan and also by the Secret Service—protection against possible danger.

de/à/par: She holds her granddaughter by the hand; the little girl takes after her, with her blue eyes, her platinum blond hair; a booklover and Francophile, she is very fond of her collection of French books, from Gustave Flaubert to Amélie Nothomb.

There's a young man who is really irritating, boring, and annoying. He has no right to use the second person singular with my dear kitty LÉO; he is not entitled to this form of address—(it's different if *droit* is followed by a noun or by a verb). A princess can never escape her golden cage; Charles Manson will never be able to escape from prison (figurative or literal).

dans/en (général/spécifique; time): Celebrities usually fly in a private jet; I am on a plane bound for Paris, I study *French Demystified* by Annie Heminway; I must master the pitfalls and the challenges of the French language before landing. In two hours, I read "Chapter 14: All about prepositions." In four hours, I'll be in Paris, prepositions polished!

There are temperamental prepositions that flirt with verbs, no formula:

de/en: Jeanne Gonzalès began to sob when she saw the portrait of Berthe Morisot by Édouard Manet; she was foaming with rage and she burst into tears. Did her rival burst into laughter, or did she laugh her head of or until she cried when she dissected this portrait?

de/au: Édouard Manet's mother loves to play the piano; to tinkle away; she escapes from daily life; she has no desire to play golf, a useless pastime, in her opinion.

Verbs have just as much fun as prepositions do, no rule:

Gervaise, Zola's laundress, does everything: she does the dishes, she does the laundry, and she washes the linens at the washhouse. Please note, this is laundering, it is not money laundering.

I glance at the wardrobe of our dear author, Alain Mabanckou, and I give him a wink.

And there are verbs that fiddle around with their prepositions:

Keep your feet on the ground: if you are ever struck by an earthquake, you fall to the ground; we don't want to put you into the ground; we fall flat on our face; we want the ground to swallow us up (from shame); we don't want to land.

The meaning of a verb can change with the introduction of a reflexive pronoun:

Eva Gonzalès, pupil of the celebrated painter Manet, overshadows her sister Jeanne; suddenly, immediately following the master's death, she slips away and dies.

We lay ourselves bare, like Ananda Devi; we are naked as the day we were born, like Amélie Nothomb at Burning Man.

We cannot neglect the position of adjectives: before or after the noun—figurative or literal.

Charles de Gaulle was big. He was a tall man—he measured 1.93 meters. In times of crisis, he really was a great man. He will remain in the annals of History.

And how about accents, the circumflex, for example?

She returned from her stay on the Île de Ré tanned; the sailors hauled a large whale on board.

And homonyms, feminine or masculine? And euphoric homonyms?

In front of his wood-burning stove, my youngest son William finds a hair from his cat Aphrodite in the crepe pan; it's not funny.

I've had just about enough: I hide under a veil, and I head off.

In verse, she writes about the life of a green worm in a glass of rosé in Ver-sur-Mer.

At my house, in the country, the ground is covered with pines, the basket is full of bread.

Erik Orsenna told me that the sea is his mother not his mayor.

That's enough! I hope that my advice hasn't spoiled your appetite for studying French!

Good luck, dear granddaughter!

With a big kiss, Lili

Lisa Ehrenkranz

(Translated by Ellen Sowchek)

EXERCICE 10·5

Port-au-Prince

Born in Port-au-Prince, Haiti, I grew up in Petit-Goâve, my childhood home. After working, as a journalist in Port-au-Prince, I had to leave my country. Living as an exile in Montreal, I had several factory jobs before writing my first novel.

Writing Montreal

Saint Louis Square is where I started writing. To me, Montreal means the typewriter. Montreal is modernity. I never thought I could write in longhand in Montreal. Montreal is also distance. Here I am, in a small room, writing about Petit-Goâve and Port-au-Prince, realizing that most of my readers do not know these cities. This affords me a certain kind of freedom. I don't need to fictionalize these cities. For my readers, they are already fictional.

A city of images

When I decided to make a film about Montreal, I wanted it to be in wintertime. I wanted a winter as severe as the summer of filming *How to Make Love*. This would enable me to look at Montreal as if I were seeing the city as it truly was, for the very first time. Because there is a winter in Montreal. I cannot go through life experiencing Montreal as a southern city. Montreal is also a Nordic city. I wanted to step closer to that winter, in an effort to tame it, to feel it, because I believe it to be the fundamental image of Montreal and Quebec. Indeed, it was Gilles Vigneault, the great Quebec poet, who once said: "I created winter from a single icicle. My land is not a land. My land is winter." I could not continue ignoring this country's winter, and I wanted that winter to be as harsh as possible. Also, in *How to Conquer America in One Night*, it seemed to me that I needed to reconcile Montreal and Port-au-Prince, the two cities that inhabit me. I wanted the film to say something—as if there were no space—about the successive paths linking the two cities. I'm talking about the gentle space between Montreal and Port-au-Prince. Truth be told, I wanted to make this film for my own pleasure. I was not surprised by the city. I wanted the image to make me see the city from a different angle, in a different way—that's what I wanted. Yes, absolutely. And I succeeded. I also wanted to include things that elude the human eye. We pass by, it's too minute. . . . Essentially, we see a city through our emotions. In fact, these emotions are so intense that I believe that watching the film will enable me to see paths traveled with new eyes, to perceive things that initially eluded me because I hastily absorbed them as feelings and not as images.

A quick tour of the city, and then boredom

I don't really look at cities. I write almost all my travel stories in a tub or in a hotel room. Not ever having to be a tourist is my dream. A tourist, for me, is an observer, a person who wants to know. I, on the other hand, do not desire to know. I desire to feel. I need a destination. I am walking in a city that I'm just getting to know; I'm on my way to meet a close friend. What I'm focusing on is the route and my desire to be at my friend's place. What I really prefer is being indoors, in a bar, in a bookstore, at a friend's place—sort of everywhere. When there is a particular destination in a city, where I am giving a lecture or promoting my books, someone usually meets me and takes me, without fail, on a short tour of the city. That is my least favorite part of the visit, because I don't like to listen to stories about a city and its history. And I definitely don't like being shown monuments or important sites. What I really like to do is to simply stroll around, noticing only the minimum that attracts my attention. This is how, after a period of incubation, I end up getting a feel for a city. I want the city to come to me. I don't want to discover it. I want it to discover me. *Translated by Zoran Minderovic.*

(From an interview with Dany Laferrière by Annie Heminway in Montreal, Canada, in February 2009, for the blog *La ville est ailleurs*, aubepine.blog.lemonde.fr, by Frédéric Antoine Brosson and Annie Heminway.)

Answer key

1 Nouns: gender and pluralization

1·1   1. Le   2. la   3. la   4. le   5. le   6. le   7. La   8. la   9. la; la   10. la

1·2   1. un   2. un   3. une   4. un   5. un   6. une   7. une   8. une
9. une   10. un

1·3   1. traductrice   2. reine   3. informaticienne   4. infirmière   5. mannequin
6. marraine   7. architecte   8. marchande   9. conceptrice   10. acheteuse

1·4   1. sa   2. sa   3. son   4. son   5. Son   6. son; sa   7. sa   8. son; sa
9. Sa   10. son

1·5   1. La   2. Le   3. La   4. La   5. Le   6. La   7. Le   8. La   9. Le
10. La   11. Le   12. Le; la   13. La   14. Le   15. Le   16. La   17. Le
18. Le   19. Le   20. La; la; la

1·6   1. une; une   2. une   3. un; un   4. Un   5. un   6. Un   7. un
8. un   9. une; un   10. Un

1·7   1. Le champ   2. Le mémoire   3. La Champagne   4. la poêle   5. La mode
6. la voix   7. Le verre   8. Le chœur   9. la voile   10. Le critique

1·8   1. Nous sommes descendus dans un petit hôtel dans le Marais.   2. Le vert que vous avez choisi pour vos rideaux est trop pâle.   3. C'est une tâche impossible.   4. Mes cousins Alain et Frédéric habitent au cœur de Paris.   5. Ils ont servi du champagne avec des amandes.   6. Il y a un ver dans ce verre.   7. Sara n'utilise que de l'encre bleue.   8. Elle a dû payer une amende de cent euros.   9. Le chant grégorien est sublime.   10. Apportez-moi un seau d'eau tout de suite!

1·9   1. bateaux   2. cas   3. prix   4. Hindous   5. animaux   6. genoux
7. locaux   8. feux   9. nounous   10. bois

1·10   1. coupe-vent   2. eaux-de-vie   3. passe-partout   4. aide-mémoire
5. gratte-ciel   6. arrière-petites-filles   7. demi-litres   8. hors-d'œuvre
9. face-à-face   10. beaux-frères

2 Accents, **h aspiré**, and capitalization

2·1   1. annonçait   2. voyageons   3. reconnaissez   4. rangèrent   5. mangea
6. as été réveillé   7. reconnaîtrais   8. finançons   9. ai reçu   10. empêchèrent

2·2   La porte étroite

—Tiens! Ma porte n'était donc pas fermée? dit-elle.

—J'ai frappé; tu n'as pas répondu, Alissa, tu sais que je pars demain?

Elle ne répondit rien, mais posa sur la cheminée le collier qu'elle ne parvenait pas à agrafer. Le mot: fiançailles me paraissait trop nu, trop brutal, j'employai je ne sais quelle périphrase à la place. Dès qu'Alissa me comprit, il me parut qu'elle chancela, s'appuya contre la cheminée . . . mais j'étais moi-même si tremblant que craintivement j'évitais de regarder vers elle.

J'étais près d'elle et, sans lever les yeux, lui pris la main; elle ne se dégagea pas, mais, inclinant un peu son visage et soulevant un peu ma main, elle y posa ses lèvres et murmura, appuyée à demi contre moi:

—Non, Jérôme, non; ne nous fiançons pas, je t'en prie . . . [. . .]

—Pourquoi?

—Mais c'est moi qui peux te demander: pourquoi ? pourquoi changer ?

Je n'osais lui parler de la conversation de la veille, mais sans doute elle sentit que j'y pensais, et, comme une réponse à ma pensée, dit en me regardant fixement:

—Tu te méprends, mon ami: je n'ai pas besoin de tant de bonheur. Ne sommes-nous pas heureux ainsi?

Elle s'efforçait en vain à sourire.

—Non, puisque je dois te quitter.

—Écoute, Jérôme, je ne puis te parler ce soir . . . Ne gâtons pas nos derniers instants . . . Non, non. Je t'aime autant que jamais; rassure-toi. Je t'écrirai; je t'expliquerai. Je te promets de t'écrire, dès demain . . . dès que tu seras parti.

—Va, maintenant!

2·3   1. La hiérarchie dans cette organisation est un jeu de hasard.   2. Le héros de ce nouveau film est un homme qui habite dans le hameau près de notre village.   3. La haine entre les deux frères est bien connue.   4. Nora est surprise par la hausse des prix du restaurant de l'hôtel.   5. Les hors-d'œuvre qu'ils ont servis étaient délicieux.   6. Est-ce que tu veux commander le homard sur le menu?   7. Le père de Carole s'est fracturé la hanche la semaine dernière.   8. Le hamac dans le jardin est un cadeau de Laurent.   9. L'hiver froid dans cette ville est le handicap principal pour nos grands-parents.   10. La honte de sa défaite est difficile à accepter.

2·4   1. Jean est belge.   2. Isabella est hongroise.   3. Les enfants de Bruno parlent français avec leurs amis et anglais avec leurs parents.   4. En Grèce, l'hiver est doux.   5. Lucie est née le 28 février.   6. Le festival de jazz a lieu du premier au quatre juillet.   7. La mer Méditerranée est moins salée que la mer Morte. 8. L'espagnol et le portugais sont les langues principales en Amérique latine.   9. Le pôle Sud est en Antarctique.   10. Quand tu fais du ski dans les Alpes, tu peux aller de France jusqu'en Slovénie.

3   Adjectives and adverbs

3·1   1. ronde   2. basse   3. cassée   4. courageuse   5. belle   6. sèche   7. violente   8. vieille 9. jeune   10. ennuyeuse

3·2   1. grosses   2. amicaux   3. murales   4. mécontents   5. fatals   6. roux   7. idéales 8. waterproof   9. normales   10. orales

3·3   1. bleus   2. déchirés   3. brisées; crevée   4. talentueux   5. arrondis; rouges   6. bleue; tranquille; grise; déchaînée   7. neufs   8. utiles; prévues; perdues   9. anciens   10. vides; remplies; multicolores; blanches

3·4   1. anti-âge   2. antivol   3. avant-coureurs   4. bien-aimées   5. bicolores   6. biodégradables 7. casse-cou   8. demi-tarif   9. interchangeables   10. subsahariens

3·5   1. roses; mauves; fuchsia   2. vert pâle   3. violettes; jaunes   4. rose orangé   5. azur   6. bleu canard; gris souris   7. ocre   8. gris   9. vert pomme   10. bleu foncé; blanche

3·6   1. i   2. j   3. f   4. g   5. h   6. c   7. a   8. b   9. e   10. d

3·7   1. nouvelle   2. mince   3. cher   4. ancienne   5. dur   6. tendre   7. maigre   8. anciennes 9. dure   10. forte

3·8   1. Antoine a un grand vélo rouge.   2. La petite maison avait un toit pointu et des volets verts.   3. Le clown avait un nez rouge et un joli canari.   4. Nous avons pêché quatre magnifiques truites.   5. Sandra collectionne les sacs ronds, roses et pailletés.   6. Ma chatte Myrtille a eu trois chatons noirs et blancs. 7. L'école a une gigantesque cour fleurie.   8. Les villes sont pleines de voitures polluantes, bruyantes et encombrantes.   9. Le nouveau minuscule appareil photo de Mathilde prend de belles photos.   10. Le jardin botanique regorge de belles plantes exotiques et rares.

3·9   1. devant   2. admirablement   3. nullement   4. la semaine prochaine   5. Apparemment 6. totalement   7. certainement   8. En ce moment   9. presque   10. près

3·10   1. Je suis moins colérique que toi.   2. Rachel est aussi maladroite que Coralie.   3. Ces casques audio sont les plus performants.   4. Ce vélo en bambou est plus écolo que ce vélo électrique.   5. C'est le blogueur le plus actif de ma région.   6. J'ai eu ce bouquet à moindre prix.   7. Tu es meilleur(e) conducteur que Morgan.   8. Cet autoportrait de Gustave Courbet est aussi magnifique que désespéré. 9. Nayla refuse d'obéir aussi énergiquement qu'Adrien.   10. Ce livre-ci se vend mieux que ce livre-là.

4 Practical pronouns

4·1   1. Enzo compte y devenir avocat.   2. Lucas y va cet après-midi.   3. Lina y prête attention.   4. N'y entrez pas! 5. Vas-y!   6. Pourquoi n'y avez-vous pas répondu?   7. Jade n'y croit pas.   8. Hugo y tient.   9. Mon cousin s'y accroche.   10. Je m'y intéresse.

4·2   1. Nous avons besoin d'un directeur qui en soit capable.   2. Les employés de notre bureau s'en plaignent. 3. Anne s'en chargera.   4. Lucas ne s'en souvient pas.   5. Natalie Dessay, qui est une grande chanteuse, en jouera aussi ce soir.   6. Un bon conseil: ne t'en mêle pas.   7. Si on licencie son assistant, Adam en sera mécontent.   8. J'aimerais bien accompagner Martin à la réception à l'ambassade du Luxembourg, mais je n'en ai pas.   9. Bien qu'elle les trouve de plus en plus envahissantes, Lilou s'en occupe avec minutie. 10. Malgré les critiques de certains de ses collègues, Mme Bréval en est fière.

4·3   1. Léo l'a choisi.   2. Jade l'a obtenu l'année dernière.   3. Emma l'a publié.   4. N'oubliez pas de le consulter!   5. Ne les acceptez pas.   6. L'as-tu vu?   7. Je l'ai finalement comprise.   8. Si tu arrives à Paris avant la fin du mois, appelle-le.   9. Je la soutiens.   10. Rendez-le à Juliette!

4·4   1. Tom lui a fait un joli cadeau.   2. Valérie leur a raconté de belles histoires.   3. Hugo, qui vient de choisir la carrière de magicien, leur annoncera sa décision demain.   4. Mme Bréval leur a expliqué le subjonctif.   5. Le petit archipel que nous voyons à l'horizon lui appartient.   6. Au risque de l'offusquer, Léna ne lui a pas donné son numéro de téléphone.   7. La classe de traduction lui a offert un carré Hermès. 8. Félix est un chien très paresseux, mais il lui apporte *Le Monde*.   9. À la différence de son ami Valentin, qui est apolitique, Antoine aime lui envoyer des analyses de la situation politique.   10. Ne lui dites rien, car elle a beaucoup de soucis à cause de sa voisine.

4·5   1. Inès le lui a envoyé.   2. Fahed le leur a recommandé.   3. Ambre leur en donne.   4. Le médecin lui en a prescrit.   5. Ethan lui en a raconté.   6. Arthur la lui a envoyée.   7. Hugo le lui dédiera. 8. Aujourd'hui, je vais lui en demander une.   9. Je lui en offrirai un, car elle s'est occupée du jardin. 10. Sans pouvoir justifier la raison, Louis veut lui en emprunter une.

4·6   1. qui   2. que   3. que   4. qui   5. que   6. qui   7. que   8. qui   9. que   10. qui

4·7   1. dont   2. dont   3. dont   4. dont   5. dont   6. dont   7. dont   8. dont   9. dont   10. dont

4·8   1. Ce dont   2. Ce à quoi   3. Ce que   4. Ce qui   5. Ce que   6. Ce dont   7. Ce qui   8. Ce dont   9. Ce que   10. Ce dont

4·9   1. Le moment où je me suis réveillé(e), je savais que quelque chose n'allait pas.   2. La boulangerie où Olivier achète son pain est près de son bureau.   3. Je n'oublierai jamais le jour où je t'ai rencontré(e). 4. Ils ne savent pas où ils vont.   5. L'été où nous avons voyagé en France, il a plu tout le temps.

5 The past tenses

5·1   1. a mangé   2. avons attendu   3. a obéi   4. ont applaudi   5. n'ai pas commandé   6. Avez; répondu   7. ont participé   8. a entendu   9. as; loué   10. n'a pas réfléchi

5·2   1. Lisa a peint un chat Maine coon.   2. As-tu vu mon sac à main?   3. Nous avons pris un verre aux Deux Magots.   4. Sacha et Juliette ont passé trois ans en Inde.   5. Pourquoi as-tu ouvert mon courrier? 6. J'ai dû partir avant la fin du spectacle.   7. Adam n'a pas lu *Les Fleurs du Mal* de Baudelaire.   8. Ma cousine Anne a couru le marathon de New York l'automne dernier.   9. Inès a offert un foulard en soie de Lyon à sa sœur.   10. Nous nous sommes assis dans l'herbe pour le pique-nique.

5·3   1. est devenue   2. êtes arrivés   3. es déjà allée   4. sommes revenues   5. ai oublié   6. est-il tombé 7. sont nées   8. n'est pas restée   9. sont sortis   10. est intervenu

5·4   1. h   2. g   3. f   4. j   5. a   6. i   7. d   8. b   9. e   10. c

5·5   1. êtes-vous rentrés   2. J'ai sorti   3. as monté   4. a descendu   5. est-elle sortie   6. sont rentrés 7. sont retournés   8. J'ai passé   9. est passé   10. sont montées

5·6   1. vendait   2. étais   3. lisais   4. prenais   5. voyagiez   6. était   7. buvait   8. neigeait 9. écrivait   10. avions

5·7 1. Nous venions de sortir quand il a commencé à pleuvoir.　2. Le match de basket-ball venait de commencer quand un incident a eu lieu.　3. Samuel marchait alors que ses cousins couraient.　4. Je battais les œufs pendant que vous mesuriez la farine.　5. Vous réserviez toujours une chambre dans le même hôtel à Saint-Malo.　6. Dans le passé, les gens utilisaient beaucoup de sel pour préserver la nourriture.　7. Caroline a vu que Diego savait danser le tango.　8. Immédiatement après l'explosion, tout le monde a pensé à une bombe.　9. Xavier et Erwan appelaient leur mère tous les jours/chaque jour.　10. Vous veniez d'être engagé(e) par cette enterprise quand le scandale a éclaté.

5·8 1. a mis　2. brûlait　3. J'ai reçu　4. volaient　5. prenais; as entendu　6. a porté; a disparu　7. voyageaient; étaient　8. lisaient; a sonné　9. avons vendu　10. était; a éclaté

5·9 1. avait tout préparé; nous sommes arrivé(e)s　2. J'ai réparé; avais cassée　3. avons mangé; avait cuisiné　4. a bu; j'avais rempli　5. ont découvert; était parti　6. a oublié; avait réclamé　7. avait manipulé; a décidé　8. avait été dévoilé; ont commencé　9. s'était bien passée; a décidé　10. aviez accepté; a changé

5·10 1. fut　2. plut　3. vécurent　4. crus　5. devint　6. mangèrent　7. guéris　8. naquis　9. admira　10. crut

5·11 1. c　2. i　3. h　4. f　5. g　6. j　7. a　8. e　9. b　10. d

5·12 Seule avec elle, je ne **savais** rien lui dire, oui si je **parlai**, je **médisais** de l'amour; j'**étais** tristement gai comme un courtisan qui veut cacher un cruel dépit. Enfin, j'**essayai** de me rendre indispensable à sa vie, à son bonheur, à sa vanité: tous les jours près d'elle, j'**étais** un esclave, un jouet sans cesse à ses ordres. Après avoir ainsi **dissipé** ma journée, je revenais chez moi pour travailler pendant la nuit, ne **dormant** guère que deux ou trois heures de la matinée.

Mais n'**ayant** pas, comme Rastignac, l'habitude du système anglais, je me **vis** bientôt sans un sou. Dès lors, mon cher ami, fat sans bonnes fortunes, élégant sans argent, amoureux anonyme, je **retombai** dans cette vie précaire, dans ce froid et profond malheur soigneusement caché sous les trompeuses apparences du luxe. Je **ressentis** alors mes souffrances premières, mais moins aiguës; je m'**étais** familiarisé sans doute avec leurs terribles crises. Souvent les gâteaux et le thé, si parcimonieusement offerts dans les salons, **étaient** ma seule nourriture. Quelquefois, les somptueux dîners de la comtesse me **substantaient** pendant deux jours. J'**employais** tout mon temps, mes efforts et ma science d'observation à pénétrer plus avant dans l'impénétrable caractère de Fœdora. Jusqu'alors, l'espérance ou le désespoir **avaient** influencé mon opinion, je **voyais** en elle tour à tour la femme la plus aimante ou la plus insensible de son sexe; mais ces alternatives de joie et de tristesse **devinrent** intolérables: je **voulus** chercher un dénouement à cette lutte affreuse, en **tuant** mon amour.

6 Future tense, conditional mood, and subjunctive mood • *Could, should, would* • *Whatever, whoever, wherever, whenever*

6·1 1. Je vais bientôt déménager à Lyon.　2. Allez-vous boire un café?　3. Alexis va étudier le mandarin l'année prochaine.　4. Lola et Charlotte vont nous rejoindre plus tard.　5. Nous allons les appeler tout de suite!　6. Le président va choisir son premier ministre.　7. Le Colisée va être nettoyé.　8. Vous allez acheter une nouvelle maison à la campagne.　9. Malo et Alice vont signer le contrat.　10. Zélie va adorer ce livre d'Olivier Adam !

6·2 1. regarderons　2. ira　3. préférerai　4. passera　5. voudront　6. apprendrez　7. sera　8. achètera　9. reviendras　10. finirai; aura

6·3 1. seraient　2. voudrait　3. habiterions　4. Pourrait-　5. aimerait　6. partirais　7. offrirait　8. Accepteriez-　9. devrait　10. aurait

6·4 1. J'aurais dû　2. n'aurait reçu　3. serions venus　4. aurait aimé　5. auriez souhaité　6. n'aurais pas attrapé　7. auraient pu　8. serait restée　9. auraient terminé　10. aurait voulu

6·5 1. e　2. j　3. h　4. g　5. i　6. a　7. d　8. c　9. b　10. f

6·6 1. habitions　2. veuille　3. sache　4. soit　5. reçoive　6. connaisse　7. pleuve　8. arrivions　9. aient　10. sois

6·7 1. Je suis content que ma sœur soit rentrée à l'université.　2. Julie n'est pas convaincue que Guillaume ait été un bon conducteur.　3. Il est surprenant que tu aies manqué le cours de danse.　4. Vous ne croyez pas que ce chien ait été obéissant.　5. Il est regrettable que je n'aie pas su changer une roue de voiture.　6. Nous souhaitons que les médicaments aient fonctionné.　7. Tu doutes que la police ait retrouvé le voleur.　8. Cela me fait plaisir que vous ayez été présents à mon mariage.　9. Ma tante est ravie que nous ayons participé au voyage.　10. Il se peut que les chercheurs aient fait une fantastique découverte.

6·8   1. Arthur est désolé que Sarah ait perdu son travail.   2. Je suis ravi(e) que nous ayons visité la cathédrale de Rouen.   3. Les parents voulaient que leur enfant grandît à la campagne.   4. Il se peut que Victoire ait déjà lu le nouveau livre de David Foenkinos.   5. Nous sommes surpris que Max ait vendu toutes ses œuvres d'art.   6. Tu crains que je n'aie pas trouvé les clés de ma voiture.   7. Il est dommage qu'Anna et Jacob aient dû quitter leur appartement.   8. Baptiste ne pensait pas que tu fusses responsable de l'accident de voiture.   9. Il est possible que j'aie mal compris vos explications.   10. Domitille est furieuse que son chat ait cassé son vase préféré.

6·9   1. pleut   2. se rende   3. soit   4. ne travaille pas   5. veuille   6. compreniez   7. soit   8. choisisse   9. conduises   10. entendions

6·10   1. h   2. j   3. i   4. f   5. b   6. a   7. c   8. e   9. d   10. g

6·11   1. Où que tu ailles, emmène-moi avec toi.   2. Quelles que soient ses idées excentriques, elle réussira.   3. Qui que vous soyez, suivez le règlement!   4. Quel que soit le cadeau, Maylis sera heureuse.   5. Quoi que tu fasses, fais-le avec amour.   6. Où que vous décidiez de vivre, choisissez une ville dans le sud de la France.   7. Quoi que vous disiez, il ne vous écoutera pas.   8. Quel que soit le prix de la bague, je l'achèterai.   9. Chaque fois que Wolfgang est à Paris, il nous rend visite.   10. Qui que vous soyez, je m'en fiche!

7   Verb transfers

7·1   1. Nous dînerons tard ce soir.   2. Jeanne, est-ce que tu peux me rendre mon stylo?   3. Il vaut mieux que vous achetiez un autre gâteau. Il y aura beaucoup d'invités à la fête.   4. J'ai si froid! Il doit y avoir une autre couverture dans l'armoire.   5. Voici le livre que tu voulais.   6. Ton frère a huit ans? Et il n'a pas peur de parler en public?   7. Il fait beau en Normandie cette semaine. Passez de bonnes vacances!   8. Combien ça coûte ? Seulement vingt euros.   9. Henri a de la chance. Il a trouvé un emploi près de son appartement.   10. Le musicien portait une casquette de base-ball bleue.

7·2   1. Bertrand ne s'est jamais remis de la mort de Paul.   2. Demain nous devons nous lever à sept heures pour prendre le petit déjeuner avec le directeur du marketing.   3. Sonia t'a emprunté beaucoup d'argent. Est-ce qu'elle te l'a rendu?   4. Il y a tant de bruit ici. Je n'ai pas entendu (compris) votre nom de famille.   5. Est-ce que vous pouvez obtenir ce roman rapidement? J'en ai vraiment besoin pour mon cours de français.   6. Descends à la station de métro du Louvre!   7. Comment est-ce que tu as attrapé la grippe en juillet sur la Côte d'Azur?   8. Nous nous réunirons une fois par mois pour parler du nouveau projet.   9. Les parents de Luc ne veulent pas qu'il rentre à la maison après 22 heures.   10. Où est-ce que le boulanger achète sa farine? Son pain est si bon.

7·3   1. Où nous emmènes-tu ce soir?   2. Il me faudra/Je mettrai/Cela me prendra deux heures pour finir cette traduction.   3. Le Grand Palais décrochera l'exposition Manet le 15 mars.   4. Prenez la première à droite!   5. Je suis sûre que Carole emportera au moins trois valises.   6. Cette place n'est pas occupée. Asseyez-vous, s'il vous plaît.   7. Enlevez vos chaussures avant d'entrer dans le temple!   8. Prends ce bracelet et mets-le dans ton sac. C'est un cadeau.   9. Les enfants aiment regarder les avions décoller à l'aéroport d'Orly.   10. Joséphine est si gentille. Elle tient de sa mère.

7·4   1. Mets ta robe rouge! Nous sortons ce soir.   2. Est-ce que vous mettrez une annonce dans le journal pour vendre votre maison?   3. Quentin a posé son ordinateur sur le bureau, puis il a déjeuné.   4. Ma collègue a mis de côté plusieurs lettres personnelles pour les lire après le travail.   5. Juliette a rangé tous les légumes dans le réfrigérateur dans un ordre parfait.   6. Mme Deville a investi tout son argent dans le nouveau magasin de sa fille.   7. Remets tout à sa place avant leur retour (avant qu'ils rentrent).   8. Jonathan a fait une demande d'aide financière.   9. Vous devez verser une caution de cinquante euros pour louer cette bicyclette.   10. J'ai mis que vous étiez employé à mi-temps.

7·5   1. Nous espérons que le temps chaud se maintiendra pendant le week-end.   2. Un policier est accusé de ne pas avoir divulgué le nom d'un complice.   3. Le mariage aura lieu dans un château du XIXe siècle.   4. Il y a plusieurs manières de tenir un crayon.   5. Pierre, comment pouvez-vous avoir de telles opinions? Vous devriez être plus objectif!   6. Tiens, tiens! Léa et Xavier à la plage!   7. Tiens l'échelle une minute!   8. Mon école a prévu une fête pour célébrer son cinquantième anniversaire.   9. Je vais essayer de trouver Madame Bernardin. Ne quittez pas!   10. Olivier gardera ces documents jusqu'à mon retour.

7·6   1. Sa famille remonte à Louis XVIII.   2. Comment est-ce que s'est passée la fête d'anniversaire de Pierre?   3. Je traversais le boulevard des Capucines quand j'ai vu Christian Lacroix!   4. Encore une assiette de cassée!   5. Louise a brûlé un feu rouge hier soir.   6. Allons à Nohant demain. Je veux visiter la maison de George Sand.   7. Nora veut retourner au Brésil l'année prochaine. Ce sera la quatrième fois.

8. Le Premier ministre de Grande-Bretagne se rendra à Dakar à la fin du mois.   9. Le bruit court que le prince a menti à sa famille.   10. Je ne peux pas enseigner aujourd'hui. Je n'ai plus de voix.

7·7   1. Je suis sûre qu'Étienne devra passer au moins une semaine à la clinique.   2. Où ranges-tu les tasses à thé?   3. Nous sommes dans un théâtre. Taisez-vous!   4. Ce pain ne se conservera pas plus de trois jours.   5. Ne me fais pas attendre!   6. Patrick ne cesse de se plaindre de tout.   7. Gardez la monnaie!   8. Tu ne peux pas l'empêcher de voir son ex-belle-mère.   9. Anne a promis de garder le secret.   10. Il oublie tout le temps d'acheter de l'huile d'olive.

7·8   1. Elle fait un chèque.   2. L'infirmière m'a fait une piqûre.   3. Cela fait trois mois que je n'ai pas rendu visite à mon grand-père.   4. Allons faire une promenade!   5. Savez-vous faire la cuisine?   6. Je ne fais que te répéter ce que j'ai entendu.   7. Son salon doit faire six mètres de largeur.   8. Je ne m'en fais pas.   9. Cela fait un an qu'elle n'a pas téléphoné à sa sœur.   10. Lucie voudrait faire une croisière.

7·9   1. activité artistique   2. sortie   3. dessert   4. cuisine   5. voyage   6. maison   7. études   8. problème   9. communication   10. sport

8   Common confusing verbs

8·1   1. Demande un rendez-vous pour vendredi matin.   2. Paul veut m'emprunter ma voiture dimanche après-midi.   3. Céline a commandé une mousse au chocolat.   4. Alexandre remet sans cesse sa carrière en question.   5. Pouvez-vous me prêter les notes que vous avez prises à la conférence?   6. Le maire de Strasbourg a ordonné la fermeture d'une discothèque.   7. L'expression est sans doute (probablement) empruntée à la langue allemande.   8. Je voudrais vous poser une question délicate.   9. Inès a emprunté une robe à sa meilleure amie, Noami.   10. Le détective a interrogé Jean et son frère.

8·2   1. Nous aurons une fête à la piscine ce soir. Est-ce que tu voudrais te joindre à nous?   2. Le Premier ministre de France et de Grande-Bretagne se rencontreront à Berlin en mai.   3. Lise, est-ce que tu veux emporter ces deux énormes valises juste pour deux jours? Est-ce que tu es folle?   4. Demandez à Pierre d'être à La Perle, rue Vieille du Temple. Je vous retrouverai (rejoindrai) vers 20 heures.   5. Apportez un joli bouquet de fleurs à Léonie!   6. Rémi déménage samedi. Est-ce que tu peux venir nous aider?   7. J'ai emmené ma nièce à l'Opéra Bastille. Elle adore Carmen.   8. Tu emménages avec Simon! Félicitations!   9. N'amène pas ton beau-frère dimanche! Je ne l'aime pas du tout.   10. L'école de Laura sait aménager l'emploi du temps des enfants pour leur donner plus de temps pour les arts et les sports.

8·3   1. Emporte   2. J'ai rencontré   3. se sont rencontrés   4. Emmène   5. ont emporté   6. Rapporte   7. nous retrouverons/nous rejoindrons   8. vous joindre à   9. déménager   10. a aménagé

8·4   1. Mélanie rendra visite à son amie Léa à Rouen cet été.   2. Pousse cette chaise contre le mur!   3. Arrête de poser des questions!   4. L'inspecteur Clouseau est si heureux aujourd'hui. Il a arrêté Sir Charles Lytton.   5. Vous devez visiter le Futuroscope à Poitiers.   6. Mon oncle fait pousser du maïs dans son jardin.   7. Les parents de Léa m'ont fait visiter leur maison.   8. Ils se sont arrêtés dans un beau village en Corrèze.   9. Nos choux-fleurs ont refusé de pousser cette année.   10. Tu a besoin de demander une autorisation pour visiter quelqu'un dans cette prison.

8·5   1. Ils ne s'attendent pas à ce que je sache jouer du piano.   2. Ne lui en veux pas! Il est fatigué et il a oublié le rendez-vous.   3. Je n'ai pas envie de sortir ce soir. 4.—Je veux te donner des oranges. Combien en veux-tu? —J'en veux trois.   5. Je ne m'attendais pas à sa réaction. J'ai été très surpris(e).   6. Je vous envie. Vous avez de la chance!   7. Je t'attendrai devant la statue de George Sand dans le jardin du Luxembourg.   8. Marion ne parle pas à son frère. Elle lui en veut. Je ne sais pas pourquoi.   9. Charlotte a des envies de fraises.   10. Je m'attends à sa victoire en mai.

8·6   1. Il manque cinq mille euros à notre organisation pour avoir une chance de gagner.   2. Édouard ne sera pas là ce soir. Il a manqué son avion.   3. Andréa ne manque pas de talent mais elle est trop timide.   4. Ma grand-mère Victorine me manque.   5. Il manque des pages à ce roman. C'est bizarre . . . 6. Je suis si triste. J'ai manqué Amélien de trois minutes.   7. Est-ce que nous te manquons?   8. Si tu manque à ton devoir, Clara te quittera.   9. Nos voyages en Bretagne me manquent.   10. Il manque des boutons à ce cardigan.

8·7   1. Savez-vous à quelle heure ils arriveront?   2. Camille a connu la faim quand elle était jeune.   3. Savez-vous conduire?   4. Je sais qu'elle est toujours en retard.   5. Les Langlois savent organiser une soirée.   6. Je suis sûre que Jonas sait la vérité.   7. Quand saurez-vous si nous pouvons leur rendre visite en

8·8   1. d   2. e   3. a   4. c   5. b

9   Using the infinitive
The causative form • The present participle • The gerund

9·1   1. J'ai vu Victorine manger un gâteau au chocolat dans son bureau.   2. Son cousin Grégoire passe son temps à jouer au basketball.   3. Mon voisin Carl passe son temps à regarder la télévision.   4. Je l'ai entendu parler dans le couloir.   5. Samuel passe ses vacances à visiter les bibliothèques à Paris.   6. En été, nous passons notre temps à voyager en Europe.   7. Carla l'a vu couper du bois dans le jardin. 8. Laurent passe son temps à apprendre des langues étrangères.   9. Elle les a entendu dire qu'ils vendraient leur maison.   10. Je le regardais dormir.

9·2   1. c   2. e   3. b   4. a   5. d

9·3   1. Ils sont assis dans l'herbe à regarder le coucher du soleil.   2. Le professeur est debout à lire un passage de *L'amant* de Marguerite Duras.   3. Xavier est allongé/étendu sur son lit à lire le dictionnaire.   4. Nous sommes étendus/allongés sur le canapé à regarder un nouveau film italien.   5. Yvon est accroupi dans le champ à ramasser des fraises.   6. Édouard est appuyé contre la porte du réfrigérateur à se demander ce qu'il va manger.   7. Lucien est appuyé contre le mur à regarder les gens danser.   8. Vous êtes debout sur une chaise à nettoyer les fenêtres.   9. La romancière est assise devant son ordinateur à penser/réfléchir à ce qu'elle va écrire.   10. Tu es accroupi dans la cuisine à essayer de réparer une porte.

9·4   1. Je ferai réparer mon ordinateur.   2. Emmanuel fera remplacer toutes les lampes dans la bibliothèque. 3. J'ai fait visiter les nouveaux bureaux de l'agence.   4. Shah Jahan a fait construire le Taj Mahal en mémoire de sa femme.   5. Fais envoyer le paquet en express!   6. Victoria fera faire une robe pour le mariage de sa cousine.   7. Faites rédiger une demande de bourse de recherche!   8. Il fera livrer les fleurs à Madame de Guermantes avant midi.   9. Vous ferez corriger les fautes d'orthographe dans votre essai.   10. Raphaël a fait laver sa voiture avant de partir en vacances.

9·5   1. en faisant   2. en nageant   3. en regardant   4. en descendant   5. Ayant accepté   6. Ignorant 7. En investissant   8. Étant   9. en faisant semblant   10. en choisissant

9·6   1. Je travaille en écoutant de la musique classique.   2. Nous parlions politique en préparant le dîner. 3. Tout en étant gentil avec elle, Paul disait toujours des choses méchantes derrière son dos.   4. Ce voyage était trop fatigant. Nous avons passé notre temps à porter des valises d'un endroit à l'autre.   5. Sachant qu'Henri était un homme dangereux, Loïc en a parlé à son patron.   6. Ayant gagné à la loterie, ils ont décidé de voyager en Asie.   7. Vos idées ne sont pas assez convaincantes.   8. Andréa a perdu ses clés en jouant au frisbee sur la plage.   9. Tout en critiquant cet écrivain, elle achetait tous ses livres.   10. Il tricotait un pull en regardant un match de football.

10   Verbs and prepositions

10·1   1. a détesté   2. sembles   3. voudrais   4. aimez   5. viendra   6. désirent   7. Laisse 8. Pourrais   9. devons   10. pensent

10·2   1. c   2. e   3. a   4. b   5. d

10·3   1. d'   2. Ø; de   3. d'; à   4. à   5. d'   6. de   7. à   8. d'   9. Ø   10. de   11. à   12. de 13. de   14. Ø   15. de   16. à   17. de; Ø   18. Ø   19. à   20. à

10·4   1. José et Julie nous ont invités à passer nos vacances avec eux.   2. Nous allons acheter un nouvel ordinateur.   3. Joël déteste faire la cuisine.   4. Sophie ne peut pas s'habituer à se lever à six heures tous les matins.   5. Ils ont réussi à rencontrer le président d'Air France.   6. Je le soupçonne de faire semblant (feindre) d'être malade ce week-end.   7. Nicolas a peur de perdre les élections.   8. Ils ont promis de nous rendre visite à la fin du mois.   9. Tu dois apprendre à jouer de la guitare.   10. J'espère que vous aimez votre nouvel appartement.

10·5   **Port-au-Prince**

Je suis né **à** Port-au-Prince **en** Haïti, j'ai grandi et passé mon enfance **à** Petit-Goâve. À Port-au-Prince, j'ai travaillé comme journaliste, puis j'ai dû quitter mon pays, exilé, pour venir **à** Montréal où j'ai travaillé **à** l'usine, **dans** différentes usines **avant** d'écrire mon premier roman.

Montréal à écrire

C'est **au** Carré Saint-Louis que j'ai commencé **à** écrire. Pour moi, Montréal, c'est la machine **à** écrire. C'est la modernité. Je n'ai jamais cru que je pourrais écrire **à** la main **à** Montréal. Montréal, c'est aussi la distance. Je suis **dans** cette petite chambre et j'écris **sur** Petit-Goâve, Port-au-Prince tout **en** sachant que les gens qui vont me lire, pour la plupart, ne connaissent pas ces villes. Ça me donne une certaine liberté. Je n'ai pas **à** fictionaliser ces villes. Elles sont déjà fictions pour mes lecteurs.

Ville en images

Quand j'ai fait un film **sur** Montréal, j'ai voulu que ce soit **en** hiver. Un hiver aussi fort que l'été du tournage de *Comment faire l'amour*. Parce que je trouvais que c'était comme si je regardais Montréal cette fois-ci pour lui-même, pour elle-même. Et **à** Montréal, il y a un hiver. Je ne peux pas passer ma vie **à** croire que Montréal est une ville du sud. Montréal, c'est aussi une ville nordique. J'ai voulu m'approcher **de** cet hiver-là et essayer **de** l'apprivoiser, essayer **de** sentir cela parce que je crois que c'est l'image fondamentale de Montréal et du Québec. D'ailleurs Gilles Vigneault, le grand poète québécois a dit: « D'un glaçon, j'ai fait l'hiver. Mon pays, ce n'est pas un pays, c'est l'hiver ». Je ne peux pas continuer **à** ne pas voir qu'il y a un hiver dans ce pays, et j'ai voulu qu'il soit le plus fort. Et dans « Comment conquérir l'Amérique **en** une nuit », il me semblait que je devais faire quelque chose qui réconcilie les deux villes et Montréal et Port-au-Prince, deux villes qui m'habitent. J'ai pensé qu'il faudrait qu'un film montre un peu les passages successifs entre les deux villes comme s'il n'y avait même pas d'espace. Je parle **de** l'espace tendre **entre** Montréal et Port-au-Prince. Donc c'était un plaisir que je voulais me faire, de faire ce film. J'ai pas été surpris **par** la ville. Je voulais que l'image me fasse voir la ville sous un autre angle, d'une autre manière, et ça je l'ai voulu. Oui, tout à fait. Et je l'ai eu. J'ai voulu aussi qu'il y ait des choses que l'être humain ne peut pas voir. C'est trop minuscule, on y passe . . . On voit la ville tellement avec nos émotions quand on y passe et que je me suis dit que peut-être je, en regardant le film, je regarderai les choses que je n'ai pas vues parce que je les avais tellement absorbées rapidement en émotion et non en images.

Un petit tour de ville et puis s'ennuie

Je ne regarde pas les villes précisément. Une grande majorité de mes chroniques à l'étranger se passent **dans** une salle de bain ou **dans** une chambre d'hôtel. Mon rêve, c'est de ne jamais être un touriste. Le touriste pour moi, c'est celui qui regarde, qui cherche à savoir. Moi, je ne cherche pas **à** savoir. Je cherche à sentir. Il me faut un but. Je marche, je vais **chez** un copain dans une ville que je viens à peine **de** connaître. C'est le trajet qui m'intéresse et le désir **d'**être chez le copain. C'est beaucoup plus les intérieurs qui me plaisent, être **dans** un bar, être **dans** une librairie, être **chez** un ami, être un peu partout. Le trajet, quand je vais dans une ville généralement—comme j'y vais comme conférencier et pour mes livres—je suis reçu par quelqu'un et qui me fait toujours faire un petit tour de la ville. C'est la partie la moins agréable pour moi parce que je n'aime pas qu'on me raconte une ville et son histoire. Et je n'aime pas qu'on me montre surtout les monuments ou les endroits importants. Ce qui m'intéresse, c'est juste **de** marcher et **de** voir le peu possible qui arrive **à** attirer ma rétine. Et finalement **par** incubation, **de** finir par sentir la ville. Je veux que la ville s'amène **à** moi. Je ne veux pas la découvrir. Je veux qu'elle me découvre.

(Extrait d'un entretien de Dany Laferrière réalisé par Annie Heminway à Montréal en février 2009, pour blog *La ville est ailleurs*, aubepine.blog.lemonde.fr de Frédéric Antoine Brosson et Annie Heminway.)

Printed in the USA
CPSIA information can be obtained
at www.ICGtesting.com
LVHW081127310824
789808LV00003B/89